CW01091267

BLOOMSBURY CHILDREN'S BOOKS
Bloomsbury Publishing Plc
50 Bedford Square, London, WC1B 3DP, UK

BLOOMSBURY, BLOOMSBURY CHILDREN'S BOOKS and the Diana logo
are trademarks of Bloomsbury Publishing Plc

First published in 2020

This book is based on the Natural History Museum exhibition *Fantastic Beasts: The Wonder of Nature*

Quotes from the book *Fantastic Beasts and Where to Find Them* © J.K. Rowling 2001
Quotes from the screenplay *Fantastic Beasts and Where to Find Them* © J.K. Rowling 2016
Quotes from the screenplay *Fantastic Beasts: The Crimes of Grindelwald* © J.K. Rowling 2018

Text © The Trustees of the Natural History Museum, London and Bloomsbury Publishing Plc 2020
Book design © Bloomsbury Publishing Plc 2020
Natural History Museum exhibits and photography © The Trustees of the Natural History Museum, London 2020
Harry Potter and Fantastic Beasts film stills and assets © Warner Bros. Entertainment Inc.
Illustrations by Olivia Lomenech Gill © Bloomsbury Publishing Plc 2017
Illustration by Jim Kay © Bloomsbury Publishing Plc 2019
Illustrations by Tomislav Tomic © Bloomsbury Publishing Plc 2020
Essays © individual essayists 2020 with the exception of
Introduction essay, A Day in the Life of a Museum Conservator, Chapter Three essay
and A Naturalist's Diary © The Trustees of the Natural History Museum, London 2020

For picture credits see page 159

The moral rights of the author, essayists and illustrators have been asserted

Wizarding World TM & © Warner Bros. Entertainment Inc.

Wizarding World characters, names and related indicia are
TM and © Warner Bros. Entertainment Inc.

Wizarding World Publishing Rights © J.K. Rowling

A catalogue record for this book is available from the British Library

Hardback ISBN 978 1 5266 2403 1
13 5 7 9 10 8 6 4 2

Paperback ISBN 978 1 5266 2404 8
13 5 7 9 10 8 6 4 2

Printed and bound in Italy

MIX
Paper from
responsible sources
FSC® C013123

FSC
www.fsc.org

To find out more about our authors and books visit www.bloomsbury.com
and sign up for our newsletters

FANTASTIC BEASTS™
THE WONDER OF NATURE

BLOOMSBURY
CHILDREN'S BOOKS
LONDON OXFORD NEW YORK NEW DELHI SYDNEY

CONTENTS

FOREWORD

By Sir Ranulph Fiennes

British explorer, holder of several endurance records, writer and poet

Sir Ranulph Fiennes OBE is described by the **Guinness World Records** *as "the world's greatest living explorer". He has summited Everest, discovered the Lost City of Ubar and is the only man alive to have travelled around the Earth's circumpolar surface. While continuing to raise millions for charity through his expeditions and global presentations, Sir Ranulph is an active conservationist.*

As an expedition leader, I've been fortunate enough to observe some of the world's most spectacular wonders. I have summited Everest and gazed down at the lower peaks of the Himalayas piercing the blanket of cloud below. I have retraced David Livingstone's famous journey in a dugout canoe up the Zambezi River to Victoria Falls. I have traversed the globe from pole to pole, mapping 1,500 kilometres of uncharted territory. When you are out in these far-flung reaches of the planet, you never know when you might encounter a fantastic beast …

During my transglobal expedition in the 1980s, myself and my friend Charlie found ourselves stranded on an ice floe. We sheltered in our freezing tent with only the odd square of flapjack and two minutes of radio access to BBC World Service news to lift our spirits each day. Luckily there was no time to get bored as we had a procession of visitors to our remote hideaway. Nineteen to be exact. Nineteen enormous, curious polar bears.

We were alerted to each arrival by snuffling and scratching around the tent, coupled with the faint smell of fish. Charlie would grab a camera, and I would snatch up a couple of pots and pans to bash together loudly. When polar bears hear a noise they do not recognise, most will move away – although it does depend, of course, on how hungry they are at the time. Before my trip, the Canadian authorities assured me that only ten per cent of Canadian polar bears would eat a human. Unfortunately when you're confronted with one, there's no time to ask whether it is part of the majority or not.

My love for exploration really began when, as a young officer in the British army, I joined the army of the Sultan of Oman. It was there that I overcame the

arachnophobia I'd lived with since being bitten by a spider as a boy in South Africa. A wolf spider jumped on my leg whilst I was camped with my mobile unit in the southern reaches of the Empty Quarter – a huge desert in the Arabian Peninsula. I was too proud in front of my soldiers to do anything but grin and brush it off. There were lots of snakes, too – some deadly. I was trained to recognise vipers, lizards and scorpions, spending many hours holed up in caves in the mountains on the Yemeni border spotting different species. Indeed, I got so good at this that while on leave in London I ended up speaking with the team at the Natural History Museum. Back then, no naturalists other than the famous botanists Theodore and Mabel Bent, in the late nineteenth century, had ever been officially allowed in Dhofar to observe scorpions and so I was happy to help out. If you visit the Museum, there's a wonderful black specimen that I am proud to have discovered. It even has my name on it in Latin – I sometimes visit and give it a stroke.

  The world is finite and there is only so much territory for an adventurer to cover, yet botanists, zoologists, glaciologists and geologists – and, of course, Magizoologists – can continue to explore areas many times over. If you take a naturalist into the middle of a jungle, there may be others who have been there before, but none would have gone equipped with the knowledge base or technology around today. Every new visitor holds the potential to discover a species or record a natural phenomenon previously unknown to science. Now *that* is true exploration.

A foot in length, of strained Snakes-skin good,
Rowling it up herein, till days fulfild,

Or nummed fingers, whose force hath been
By heat extending what cold band did hold.

The wounds that come by the biting or stinging of this Serpent, are not great, but very small, and scarcely to be discerned outwardly, yet the accidents that follow, are like to those which ensue the bitings of Vipers, namely, inflamation, and a lingering death. The cure thereof must be the same which is applyed unto the sting of Vipers. And peculiarly I finde not any medicine serving for the cure of this poyson alone, except that which *Pliny* speaketh of, namely Coriander drunk by the patient, or laid to the sore.

It is reported by *Galen* and *Grevinus*, that if a woman with childe do chance to go over one of these Double-headed Serpents dead, she shall suffer abortment, and yet that they may keep them in their pockets alive without danger in boxes. The reason of this is given by *Grevinus*, because of the vapour ascending from the dead Serpent, by a secret antipathy against humane nature, which suffocateth the childe in the mothers womb. And thus much for this Serpent.

Of the DRAGON.

AMong all the kindes of Serpents, there is none comparable to the Dragon, or that affordeth and yeeldeth so much plentiful matter in History for the ample discovery of the nature thereof: and therefore herein I must borrow more time from the residue, then peradventure the Reader would

CHAPTER ONE

FANTASTIC BEASTS™

THE WONDER OF NATURE

"... from darkest jungle to brightest desert,
from mountain peak to marshy bog ..."

Newt Scamander

FANTASTIC BEASTS
AT THE MUSEUM

By Louis Buckley

Lead Curator of the Fantastic Beasts exhibition at the Natural History Museum

The Natural History Museum in London is an extraordinary treasure trove of the natural world. Some eighty million animals, plants, fossils and minerals are carefully stored within its ornate walls, which have been welcoming visitors for almost 140 years. But while many of our exhibits may already appear stranger than fiction – it is not every day that you wander past a *Stegosaurus* skeleton or a preserved giraffe – few visitors step inside the Museum expecting an encounter with a unicorn or a sea monster, let alone a Mooncalf, Erumpent or Bowtruckle.

In taking on an exhibition dedicated to the magical beasts of the Wizarding World, we therefore had to think very carefully about how to balance our critical, scientific approach to curation with the storytelling power of the page and screen. Most importantly, we had to ask ourselves, how should a museum with a proud tradition of studying evidence from the natural world go about researching an exhibition featuring creatures that exist solely in stories, myths and the imagination?

Our answer was to connect the curious creatures of *Fantastic Beasts and Where to Find Them* to the splendour of real-life nature, and to celebrate all of the astonishing parallels between them. We are not experts in how J.K. Rowling's magical animals were brought to life on-screen, fascinating though that is, so our approach was to comb the Museum's collections and look for stories that are every bit as fantastic, remarkable, strange and spectacular as anything written in Newt Scamander's field notes.

We spoke to dozens of the more than 300 scientists who work at the Natural History Museum and, with their guidance, visited hundreds of specimens that are stored behind the scenes. We opened cupboards filled with countless jars of fish of every shape and size; examined battered packing crates, nets and explorers' sketchbooks from long-past expeditions; carefully turned the pages of 500-year-old books printed with images of weird and wonderful beasts; pulled out drawers

containing enormous moths and spiders the size of dinner plates; peered at tiny wasps barely visible to the naked eye; and wandered through cavernous storerooms filled with antelopes, zebras and the bones of elephants and whales.

Many of the taxidermy and preserved animals in the Natural History Museum's stores and displays are more than one hundred years old. While Museum scientists still collect animals from the wild today, they do so in very small numbers and with careful consideration for endangered and protected species. None of this contemporary collecting is done solely for display. Its aim is to gather vital information that can help us better understand – and protect – the natural world.

Throughout our research we also looked to Newt Scamander himself, esteemed Magizoologist and author of *Fantastic Beasts and Where to Find Them* and, of course, the star of the Warner Bros. film series. Newt reminded us of the many intrepid naturalists and explorers, past and present, who have worked here at the Natural History Museum – boldly setting out across the globe to better understand the world's animals and plants, and to discover how the history of life on Earth has unfolded.

Our exhibition begins with Newt and a look at the origins of some of the best-known beasts that he describes in his A–Z of magical creatures. While many fantastic beasts are of J.K. Rowling's own invention, such as the tree-dwelling Bowtruckle and the mischievous Niffler, many others are borrowed from myths and folk tales that stretch back hundreds or even thousands of years. Picture the fierce griffin, with the head, wings and forelegs of a giant eagle and the body of a lion; the mysterious, seahorse-like Hippocampus; and the majestic, plumed phoenix rising out of burning flames. While it is impossible to trace exactly where these or the likes of dragons, unicorns, mermaids and sea monsters might have come from, some researchers have suggested that they may have been inspired by people uncovering the bones of dinosaurs and other extinct animals, such as the huge mammoths and woolly rhinoceroses that roamed the Earth during the last Ice Age.

Complicating matters further is the fact that many of the beasts that are now staples of fantasy books, films and games were once very much believed to be real animals. As Newt himself notes:

"A glance through Muggle art and literature of the Middle Ages reveals that many of the creatures they now believe to be imaginary were then known to be real."

You can see evidence of this for yourself in the beautiful engravings that fill medieval books, including the dragons and unicorns found inside the wonderful *A History of Four-Footed Beasts and Serpents* (published in 1658) and from objects such as the 900-year-old carved narwhal tusk (*Monodon monoceros*), which was once believed to be a precious and powerful unicorn horn, but is now known to be the overgrown tooth, or 'tusk', of an Arctic whale.

However, science has also shown us that some of the 'monsters' of myth and

legend do exist, at least in a manner of speaking. The discovery of the colossal squid (*Mesonychoteuthis hamiltoni*) in the 1920s revealed a giant of the deep that was every bit as incredible – and potentially terrifying – as any sea monster. This magnificent creature has never been observed in its natural habitat as it lurks in the remote, icy depths of the Antarctic and Southern Oceans. Stretching up to fourteen metres (forty-six feet) in length, it is even bigger than its famous relative, the giant squid (*Architeuthis dux*), which can be found in oceans around the world and, of course, splashing playfully in the black lake at Hogwarts School of Witchcraft and Wizardry.

Following Newt's lead, the second part of our exhibition takes Muggles on an adventure out into the wild. Newt himself "visited lairs, burrows and nests across five continents", and in turn, we bring together animals from all across the planet with abilities or features that rival any of the "curious habits" of the beasts detailed in his great work. From the rainforests of Central Africa we quietly observe the okapi, a relative of the giraffe that is so shy and elusive that it lived undetected by Western scientists until the early 1900s. Paired with this fascinating animal is the magical Mooncalf, a silvery creature that emerges from its burrow only at the full moon to survey the world with its large, saucer-like eyes. Diving down to the ocean depths, we peer into the darkness, hoping to catch a glimpse of a shrimp-like animal called *Cystisoma*. With its transparent body, *Cystisoma* can vanish from sight almost as effectively as Newt's Demiguise, Dougal, although it is not known to share his taste for sweets or handbags. And climbing up high into the Himalayas we find the Royle's pika, a rabbit-like creature that, like the Niffler with its hoard of shiny coins and jewels, gathers a larder of flowers, grasses and mosses to help it survive when food is scarce.

As these few examples show, there is an extraordinary diversity of life on Earth for both Muggles and wizards to discover. But while Newt's book contains eighty-one different magical creatures, scientists have so far recorded eight million animal species, with more wonders being discovered every year. In 2019 alone, scientists at the Natural History Museum identified 412 new species ranging from snakes and lizards to wasps, butterflies, moths and beetles. Sadly, we also know that many of the world's animals, plants, fungi and other organisms are threatened by extinction, often disappearing soon after they are first recorded, or even before we notice them at all.

Given this stark reality, we felt that it was only right to focus the final section of our exhibition on the huge threats faced by many incredible creatures – and, indeed, by nature as a whole – from global heating, pollution, loss of habitat, and the many other pressures that result from human actions. Newt himself is fiercely driven by the desire to protect and care for endangered creatures and this impulse is ever-present throughout the Fantastic Beasts film series. The Magizoologist's trip to New York at the start of the first film is intended to return Frank, the majestic Thunderbird, to his home in the deserts of Arizona, while in the memorable scene where Newt's Muggle friend Jacob Kowalski first encounters the slimy tentacles of a Graphorn, Newt explains that he is the last hope for these endangered beasts:

"So they're the last breeding pair in existence. If I hadn't managed to rescue them, that could have been the end of Graphorns — for ever."

In a world where scientists are warning that up to a million species of animal and plant could go extinct in the next ten years, we felt it vital to showcase a few of the starkest, most moving and inspiring stories of animals that are under threat – and the people who, like Newt, are doing everything they can to save them. For some of the animals in the exhibition, it is already too late – the beautiful Caspian tiger (*Panthera tigris virgata*) vanished from Central Asia in the 1970s, its habitat eaten up by farmland and expanding towns, leading to ever greater conflict with humankind. The vaquita (*Phocoena sinus*), meanwhile, is likely to share the Caspian tiger's fate, despite the best efforts of conservationists in Mexico and the USA. This tiny porpoise – a relative of whales and dolphins – has been reduced to fewer than twenty individuals in its home waters in the Gulf of California. Endangered by illegal fishing, a trade that also harms everything from whales and sharks to sea turtles, the vaquita's tragedy is that it is likely to be declared extinct during the lifespan of our exhibition.

Although it also began with a sad tale of long-term decline, one of the most inspiring stories in our exhibition is that of the kākāpō (*Strigops habroptila*). Reduced to just fifty-one animals in the mid-1990s, this flightless parrot, with vibrant green feathers, a loud booming call and a charming waddling walk, is now on an upward trajectory thanks to the extraordinary efforts of the New Zealand government, scientists, volunteers and indigenous communities, who use everything from drones and radio transmitters to keep it safe from predatory cats, rats and stoats that hunt the bird and its eggs. The kākāpō is an uplifting example of the dedication, passion and achievements possible when people come together to protect fantastic beasts.

We hope you enjoy our exhibition – and this book – and that you take from them the inspiration to care for and cherish the natural world at a time when it needs our protection more than ever before. I think it most fitting that we end with Newt's explanation for why

Magizoology matters, which seems as important now as when he, guided by the pen of J.K. Rowling, first wrote these words in 1927. Why, Newt asks, do we try to care for and protect the fantastic beasts that share our planet?

"The answer is, of course: to ensure that future generations of witches and wizards enjoy their strange beauty and powers as we have been privileged to do."

A DAY IN THE LIFE OF A MUSEUM CONSERVATOR

By Lorraine Cornish
Head of Conservation at the Natural History Museum

Inside every museum is a hidden world of amazing objects that are stored on shelves or in drawers awaiting their time to be seen and studied by experts or placed on display for an exhibition. Conservators work behind the scenes to make sure these treasures are preserved and cared for.

The Conservation Centre at the Natural History Museum is a series of large spaces that are rather like a hospital, but the 'patients' are specimens from the Museum collections. Any treatments carried out are recorded and are added to each specimen record in a similar way to having a medical record. No two days are ever the same and many different types of objects, ranging from large mammals to tiny insects, pass through the doors. Enter the conservator's world for a day and discover more about their fascinating work and the specimens they care for.

At the start of the day

I arrived early to check progress on a large and rather beautiful specimen of a Caspian tiger, which was going on display. The tiger had been carefully wheeled into the conservation centre from the collection store and we had taken detailed photographs and made notes to record its condition. The specimen had been purchased from a taxidermy company back in 1927. These amazing tigers were once found across Central Asia but were driven to extinction in the 1970s as humans replaced their habitat with farms and cities. It is the only complete taxidermy specimen of this type of tiger that we have in the collection, which makes it extra special. Before starting, we had written a treatment outline and talked through plans with the mammal curator who looks after our tiger collection. The tiger needed a clean and some whiskers made. Its fur was gently dry-cleaned with brushes and sponges, which removed dust from the surface.

The next job was to replicate the missing whiskers, which is not an easy task. Conservators often face this sort of problem, working out how to fabricate replacements that will look very similar to the real thing. All the materials we use need to be chemically inert and stable to help preserve the specimen. Nikki, one of our conservators, created false whiskers by inserting a thick nylon thread into catheter tubing. She used a heated spatula to flatten them and to make the whisker shape and then she cut them to various lengths with a scalpel. The 'whiskers' were painted to look like the real thing. Different length false whiskers were created to match the existing whiskers on the other side of the tiger's face. Using a magnifying glass, it was easy to see the small holes where the original whiskers would have been and to gently glue the new false ones into place.

Maintaining specimens is a painstaking process.

After lunch

Later in the day I met up with Cheryl, who was working on a scary-looking Colombian lesserblack tarantula. This magnificent spider came to us back in 1875, and Cheryl's job was to carry out an invisible repair on one of its legs, which had previously been held loosely in place with a pin. We also noted that some of the spider hairs were loose in the bottom of the container. These are potentially hazardous as they can cause swelling and itching if they come into contact with the skin, so care was needed. Repairing the leg involved using a special type of Japanese tissue that is made from very strong fibres, plus a special glue mix. A tiny amount of the tissue and glue was gently pushed into the hollow leg while the pin was still in place. With the help of some tweezers, this secured both parts of the leg.

Late afternoon

Finally, I met up with Arianna, who was repairing the ears of a Canada lynx after giving it a gentle clean. This impressive specimen came to us from Alaska back in 1904. The lynx has very good hearing and has special tassels of fur on its ears to pick up even more sound. Some of the tassels were missing or damaged and needed to be repaired. Using a crafting technique called felting, Arianna was able to replace the missing tassels. She used a thin fabric called Reemay as a base support and then poked pieces of dark-coloured wool into the fabric with a sharp needle. This patch was then attached to each of the ears using special glue.

It takes many hours to complete all the cleaning and repairs, but the work does ensure that these specimens will look their best when they go on show to the public.

CHAPTER TWO

MYTH AND LEGEND

"The unicorn is a beautiful beast found throughout the forests of northern Europe."

Newt Scamander

MYTH AND LEGEND

Dr Helen Scales

Science writer, broadcaster and marine biologist

*Dr Helen Scales is a marine biologist, writer and broadcaster. Among her books are the bestseller **Spirals in Time** and a Ladybird book about octopuses. She divides her time between Cambridge in England and the wild French coast of Finistère.*

If Newt Scamander invited me to climb into his case, the first thing I would do is jump in the pool and go for a swim with the kelpie. I'm sure I'd feel safe under Newt's watchful eye, but if it were an encounter in the wild I would probably be more careful – in mythology, kelpies have a nasty reputation for drowning and eating people. The Celtic kelpies are joined by herds of other mythical water horses, like the mischievous nuggles from the Shetland Isles and the sinister bäckahäst of Scandinavia, which appear near rivers on foggy days, luring riders to climb on, before dragging them underwater. It's thought that the folk tales of menacing horses may have sprung from dark, deep lakes and fast-flowing rivers as a warning to children to stay away.

Glimpses of all sorts of real animals have inspired a menagerie of mythical beasts. Many have swum through the oceans and peeped above the waves only to swiftly disappear again, leaving salt-encrusted mariners pondering what they saw. That could be how oarfish became sea serpents, and giant squid transmogrified into the kraken. Dragons appear in myths and legends all around the world, usually imagined as an assortment of body parts from familiar animals – snakes and birds, fishes and turtles, crocodiles, lizards and lions. Newt's kelpie is especially close to my heart because it looks to me like a weed-encrusted seadragon. These are not in fact dragons, but unusual fish called leafy seadragons that live hidden away along the southern shores of Australia, disguising themselves among the fronds of seaweed forests. It seems unlikely that the Australian seadragons were the inspiration behind the horse myths – and I don't suppose one has ever drowned a human – but they certainly fit the descriptions of these watery equine spirits.

Seahorses are close relatives of seadragons, and they have spawned their own myths and legends. I will always remember the first time I saw a wild

Pl. XXVI.   T. 2. P. 256.

Denys-Montfort, del.   E. Voysard S.

LE POULPE COLOSSAL.

seahorse. With its tiny equine head, the swivelling eyes of a chameleon and curling monkey's tail, it could so easily have drifted from the pages of a book of fairytales. No wonder when fishermen in ancient Greece found seahorses tangled in their nets, they thought these were the offspring of the Hippocampus, the fabled half-horse half-fish that served as the sea god Poseidon's mighty steeds. Newt lists the Hippocampus in his bestiary as a species "usually to be found in the Mediterranean", although he also notes that a blue roan specimen was caught and subsequently domesticated by merpeople off the coast of Scotland in the late 1940s. It appears that the Hippocampus is legendary throughout the wizarding world – so much so that its name, *Hippocampe*, appears inscribed beneath the magnificent domed ceiling of the French Ministry of Magic alongside other iconic magical beasts such as the centaur and the dragon.

Even a dead seahorse keeps its enigmatic shape, its body encased in a suit of armour rather than scales. That could explain why for centuries people have believed in their magical and curative powers. Find one washed up on a beach and you hold in your hand an intricate creature from the unseen deep. Dried seahorses have long been used as lucky amulets and talismans to defend against evil spirits. In ancient Rome, seahorse ashes even served as a poison and a cure for baldness. Swallow an ancient Chinese water-fairy pill, made from seahorses mixed with red speckled spiders, and supposedly you'll be able to breathe underwater, just as Harry Potter does after eating Gillyweed in the Triwizard Tournament. Sadly people today still believe in the healing powers of seahorses – even though scientists have found no proof they contain any therapeutic chemicals, and the trade in traditional Asian medicines is putting populations of these curious fish in danger.

Many fantastic beasts have made themselves known not so much from sightings glimpsed in the wild but from the control these supernatural beings hold over the world. If you anger a giant Japanese catfish, it will stir earthquakes and tsunamis, while Thunderbirds such as the specimen named Frank that Newt once rescued from captivity in Egypt throw lightning bolts from their beaks and thunderclaps from their wings. Indeed, Thunderbirds are so powerful and intelligent that Newt entrusted Frank with a vital mission during his time in New York. Just when the wizarding world was on the brink of being exposed, he released the Thunderbird to disperse a potion as rainfall over the city. This erased the memories of all non-magical people and protected the status quo.

Some real animals, meanwhile, offer proof that ancient legends must be true. Unicorns, as it turned out, had been hiding beneath the Arctic sea ice in the form of buck-toothed narwhals, at least as far as the medieval traders who dealt in their valuable horns were concerned. And when Christopher Columbus saw manatees, otherwise known as sea cows, swimming through the tropical Caribbean seas, they were the mermaids he had heard so much about (although perhaps not quite as beautiful as he was expecting).

Merpeople appear in stories spanning the globe and stretching back thousands of years. Among hordes of amphibious folk are Melusine from European medieval tales; Iara from Brazil; Sedna from Inuit legends; and the ningyo of Japan, which are sometimes depicted with the whole body of a fish and just a human's head. Mami Wata is a pan-African water spirit often associated with West African manatees, and in some places she is still worshipped and revered. With so many merman and mermaid myths, there seems to be something irresistible about the idea of people who can live both on land and in the water, crossing the divide between two parts of our world and connecting us to its mysterious, hidden depths.

Today, the latest generation of merpeople are the scientists who explore the underwater realm with the help of small submarines and diving robots that can reach the greatest depths and peer into places where nobody has looked before. When they explore the deep ocean, they are able to glimpse creatures that would fit right into Newt's menagerie. There are strawberry-coloured squid with one giant yellow eye, acrobatic worms that throw glowing green fireworks when they're scared, sea spiders the size of dinner plates, sharks that live for centuries, and herds of sea cucumbers that roam the abyss like pale, miniature pigs with spiny crabs riding on their backs. As long as people keep looking, there will always be more to find … and more tales to tell of the world's most fantastic beasts.

INTRODUCTION

From fire-breathing dragons to mysterious mountain yetis, and magnificent phoenixes to magical unicorns, mythical creatures have captured our imaginations since the beginning of time.

Tales of encounters with these fantastic beasts have entertained generations, thrilling and terrifying in equal measures. Some have inspired hope and wonder, but more often they have provoked fear and misunderstanding. These ancient myths were used to explain the mysteries of nature, serving as portents of momentous or calamitous events. Generations of cultures worldwide have passed down the stories of these magical creatures, from the traditional legends of ancient peoples to the contemporary popular myths of today. Some mythical beasts, such as the yeti or the famous Scottish Loch Ness Monster, continue to be 'spotted' in their natural snowy-mountain or watery-lake habitats, and are still searched for.

Everywhere you go you will find evidence of these iconic beasts – artefacts, tapestries and paintings in museums and galleries; gargoyles and statues on churches and grand buildings; folk tales, epic poems and songs; incredible CGI images in films.

And what about the real fossil remains and living animals that inspired these myths? Picture blinking, scaly reptiles; strange sea creatures with terrifying tentacles or long fish-like tails; mysterious horse-like beasts with twisted horns. These familiar animals became dragons, krakens, mermaids and unicorns.

Just as many mythical creatures were killed or exploited in the wizarding world for the magical powers of their feathers or horns, many real species in our world have been hunted and exploited to the point of extinction. It is important to understand why this is happening, to educate and inform ourselves about the needs and rights of all of nature's incredible creatures, and the impact our actions have on them and their living environments. Too many animals are being added to the list of endangered species. We must act now to save and protect these valuable members of our complex, interrelated ecosystems. Whether magical or real, all creatures should be permitted to survive and thrive in their natural habitats. In the past, people interpreted never-before-seen specimens as creatures of legend. Now we have a wealth of information and research readily available, and we can learn so much more about the amazing real animals that inspired the magic of the myths.

POISSONS, ECREVISSES ET CRABES (FISHES, CRAYFISH AND CRABS), 1718–1719
LOUIS RENARD, ILLUSTRATED BY SAMUEL FALLOURS
The Natural History Museum

A glance through Muggle art and literature of the Middle Ages reveals that many of the creatures they now believe to be imaginary were then known to be real. The dragon, the griffin, the unicorn, the phoenix, the centaur – these and more are represented in Muggle works of that period…

Fantastic Beasts and Where to Find Them

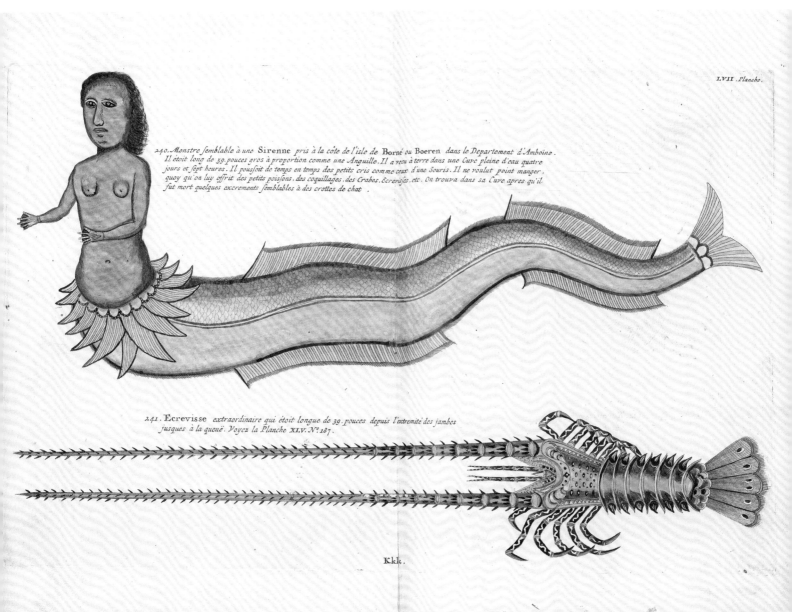

LVII. Planche.

240. Monstre semblable à une Sirenne pris à la côte de l'isle de Borné ou Boeren dans le Departement d'Amboine. Il étoit long de 59 pouces gros à proportion comme une Anguille. Il a vecu à terre dans une Cuve pleine d'eau quatre jours et sept heures. Il poussoit de temps en temps des petits cris comme ceux d'une Souris. Il ne voulut point manger, quoy qu'on luy offrit des petits poissons, des coquillages, des Crabes, Ecrevisses, etc. On trouva dans sa Cuve apres qu'il fut mort quelques excrements semblables à des crottes de chat.

241. Ecrevisse extraordinaire qui étoit longue de 39 pouces depuis l'extremité des jambes jusques à la queuë. Voyez la Planche XLV. N°. 187.

Kkk.

TALES OF OLD

Stories of dragons and other giant reptiles have been around since at least the time of the ancient Greeks. In 1335 a strange elongated skull was found in a pit near the city of Klagenfurt, Austria. It was thought to have come from a two-legged flying dragon known as the *Lindwurm*. According to the legend, this mythical beast was rumoured to have terrorised the local people and was slain in the thirteenth century, before the city was founded. Scientists later identified the skull as belonging to a long-extinct mammal of the Ice Age, the woolly rhinoceros.

DEFENCE AGAINST DRAGONS

In the Harry Potter film series, a dragon skeleton is seen hanging from the ceiling of the Defence Against the Dark Arts classroom at Hogwarts. Its skull has spines, spikes and sharp teeth, which are typical features of many of the dragon breeds that appear in the Wizarding World created by J.K. Rowling.

DRAGON SKULL
PROP FROM THE HARRY POTTER FILMS
Warner Bros.

DRAWING OF THE COMMON WELSH GREEN DRAGON (ETCHING WITH HAND COLOURING)
OLIVIA LOMENECH GILL
Bloomsbury

Woolly rhinoceroses (*Coelodonta antiquitatis*) lived in Europe and Asia from 500,000 to 14,000 years ago.

An imposing statue of the *Lindwurm* dragon perches on a monument in the city of Klagenfurt, Austria. It dates from 1590, and its huge head was modelled on a woolly rhinoceros's skull.

COMMON WELSH GREEN DRAGON ➤

Olivia Lomenech Gill produced this artwork for the Illustrated Edition of *Fantastic Beasts and Where to Find Them*. Where possible, Lomenech Gill based the magical beasts on real animals, using museum collections as inspiration. This included a visit to the Natural History Museum in London. While she used lizards as a reference for dragons, Lomenech Gill was also influenced by another iconic dragon – Smaug of J.R.R. Tolkien's *The Hobbit*. Fleur Delacour takes on the Common Welsh Green dragon in the first task of the Triwizard Tournament in *Harry Potter and the Goblet of Fire*.

" ... this breed is among the least troublesome of the dragons, preferring, like the Opaleye, to prey on sheep and actively avoiding humans unless provoked. "

Fantastic Beasts and Where to Find Them

DRAGONS

Dragons sit alongside real animals such as giraffes and rhinos in this 360-year-old book of natural history. The author, clergyman Edward Topsell, describes dragons as a type of serpent and includes several varieties from across the globe. Some slither like snakes on their bellies, while others have legs and wings. Throughout the history of dragons, these mighty beasts have been seen as both fearsome and kind, intelligent creatures. The dragons of Chinese culture are powerful, benevolent and believed to bring good fortune; the dragons of Western cultures are often seen as evil beasts that killed, created chaos and guarded treasure.

THE HISTORY OF FOUR-FOOTED BEASTS AND SERPENTS, 1658
EDWARD TOPSELL
The Natural History Museum

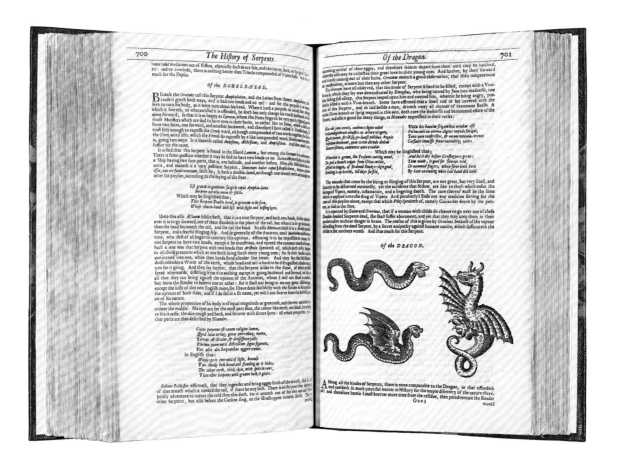

"*Probably the most famous of all magical beasts ... The female is generally larger and more aggressive than the male, though neither should be approached by any but highly skilled and trained wizards.*"

Fantastic Beasts and Where to Find Them

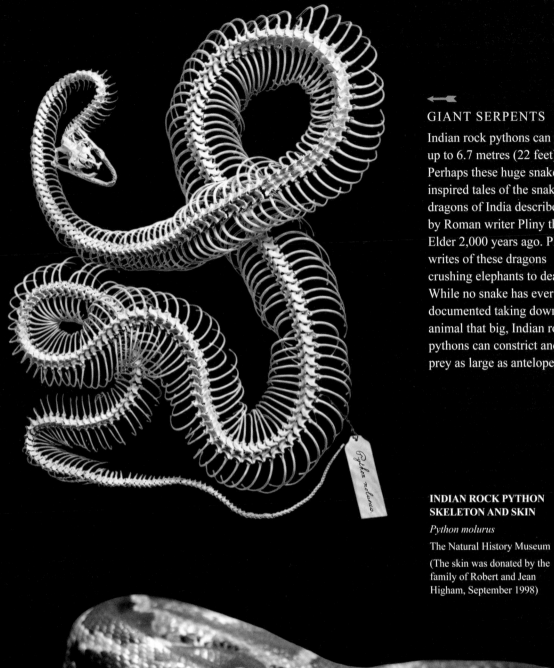

GIANT SERPENTS

Indian rock pythons can grow up to 6.7 metres (22 feet) long. Perhaps these huge snakes inspired tales of the snake-like dragons of India described by Roman writer Pliny the Elder 2,000 years ago. Pliny writes of these dragons crushing elephants to death. While no snake has ever been documented taking down an animal that big, Indian rock pythons can constrict and kill prey as large as antelope.

INDIAN ROCK PYTHON SKELETON AND SKIN

Python molurus
The Natural History Museum
(The skin was donated by the family of Robert and Jean Higham, September 1998)

THE DRAGON KING OF HOGWARTS

Based on the skull and bone fragments found in 2004, scientists believe this is what *Dracorex hogwartsia* (named in celebration of Hogwarts School of Witchcraft and Wizardry) might have looked like. Unlike the magical Hungarian Horntail of the wizarding world, this huge beast was probably a plant eater and likely lived in a small herd, like other pachycephalosaur dinosaurs that roamed the Earth 140 to 66 million years ago.

Dracorex hogwartsia **HEAD RECONSTRUCTION**
The Children's Museum of Indianapolis, USA

A SKULL FOR FIGHTING

Everything we know about *Dracorex hogwartsia* comes from this skull and a few fragments of bone. While mythical dragons are best known for attacking with fire, the flat-topped skull of *Dracorex* suggests these dinosaurs fought each other by pushing their heads together. The spiky ridges might have helped prevent their heads from slipping.

Dracorex hogwartsia **SKULL, ABOUT 67 TO 66 MILLION YEARS AGO**
HELL CREEK FORMATION, SOUTH DAKOTA, USA
The Children's Museum of Indianapolis, USA

"Supposedly the most dangerous of all dragon breeds, the Hungarian Horntail has black scales and is lizard–like in appearance… The Hungarian Horntail feeds on goats, sheep and, whenever possible, humans."

Fantastic Beasts and Where to Find Them

PAINTING OF THE HUNGARIAN HORNTAIL DRAGON (ETCHING WITH WATERCOLOUR)
OLIVIA LOMENECH GILL
Bloomsbury

CHINESE 'DRAGON'

Could this little alligator have inspired stories of great Chinese dragons? Some texts describe Chinese dragons digging burrows, breathing out rain clouds and sleeping in pools during winter. Similarly, the Chinese alligator hibernates underground, and in spring steam rises from males' nostrils as they bellow to attract a mate.

CHINESE ALLIGATOR
Alligator sinensis
The Natural History Museum

'DRACO DORMIENS NUNQUAM TITILLANDUS'

The Latin motto of Hogwarts School of Witchcraft and Wizardry means 'Never tickle a sleeping dragon'.

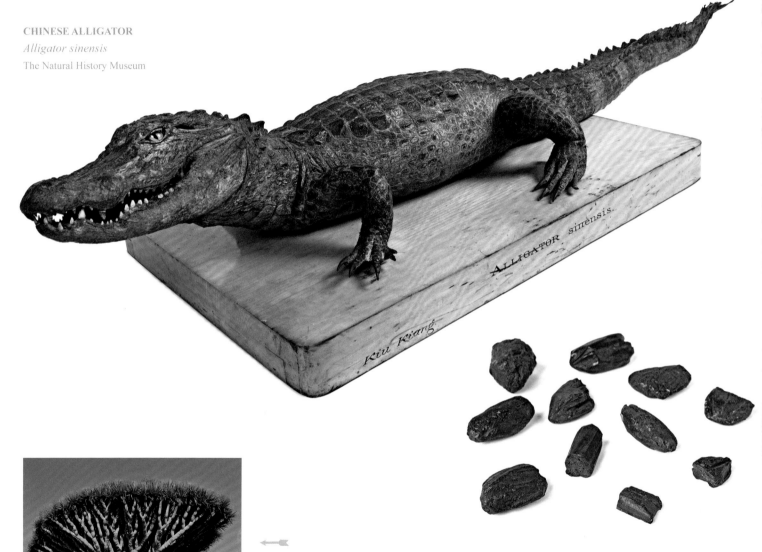

Dracaena cinnabari or 'dragon's blood tree' is one of the main sources of dragon's blood resin, which is used to make many items, from incense to paints and dyes. This unusual tree, with its amazing umbrella-like appearance, is found only on the island of Socotra, off the coast of Yemen.

A SAMPLE OF DRAGON'S BLOOD
FROM THE COLLECTION OF HANS SLOANE
The Natural History Museum

> *" The Fireball gained its name for the mushroom–shaped flame that bursts from its nostrils when it is angered."*
>
> *Fantastic Beasts and Where to Find Them*

This serpent-like dragon, depicted on the Nine-Dragon Screen in the Forbidden City in Beijing China, shows some of the typical features of a Chinese dragon. These include a long, scaled body, four legs, no wings, and a strong connection with water.

The Chinese alligator is one of the most endangered crocodilians. The decline in its numbers is due mainly to habitat loss, pollution and hunting. However, conservation programmes (including captive breeding) are underway to try to increase the numbers of this small, rare alligator.

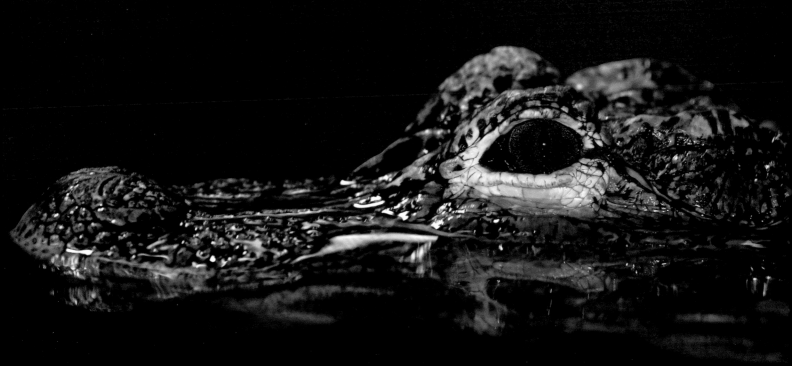

MERPEOPLE

People have claimed sightings of mermaids throughout history, and the appearance of these mysterious sea creatures has varied from culture to culture. The ancient Greek sirens had bird bodies and human heads, and the selkies of Scotland were seals that changed into human form on land. Mermaids were often associated with misfortune and death, luring sailors off course with their sweet songs and beauty. Some folklore, however, tells of kind, benevolent creatures who save lives and fall in love.

THE MERPEOPLE OF HOGWARTS

Harry Potter sees a beautiful stained-glass window featuring a mermaid in the prefects' bathroom at Hogwarts in the film adaptation of *Harry Potter and the Goblet of Fire*. When Harry later encounters real merpeople in the black lake, he finds that their greyish skin, wild green hair and broken teeth look nothing like the mermaid from the window.

STAINED-GLASS WINDOW FEATURING A MERMAID

REPLICA OF A PROP FROM THE HARRY POTTER FILM *HARRY POTTER AND THE GOBLET OF FIRE*, 2005

Warner Bros.

Glimpses of floating manatees while out at sea and eerie whale song heard from ships may have inspired the myths of mermaids. In 1493 Christopher Columbus reported seeing three mermaids during his first journey to what we now call the Americas. He noted that they rose out of the sea and had human-like faces. Based on the location of his sighting – near modern-day Haiti in the Caribbean – it is possible that Columbus actually saw three American manatees (*Trichechus manatus*). Manatees, also known as sea cows, are marine mammals. They sometimes perform 'tail stands' as they float in shallow water. Their forward-facing eyes give them a human-like appearance.

"Merpeople exist throughout the world, though they vary in appearance almost as much as humans. Their habits and customs remain as mysterious as those of the centaur ..."

Fantastic Beasts and Where to Find Them

**PAINTING OF MERPEOPLE
(ETCHING WITH WATERCOLOUR)**
OLIVIA LOMENECH GILL
Bloomsbury

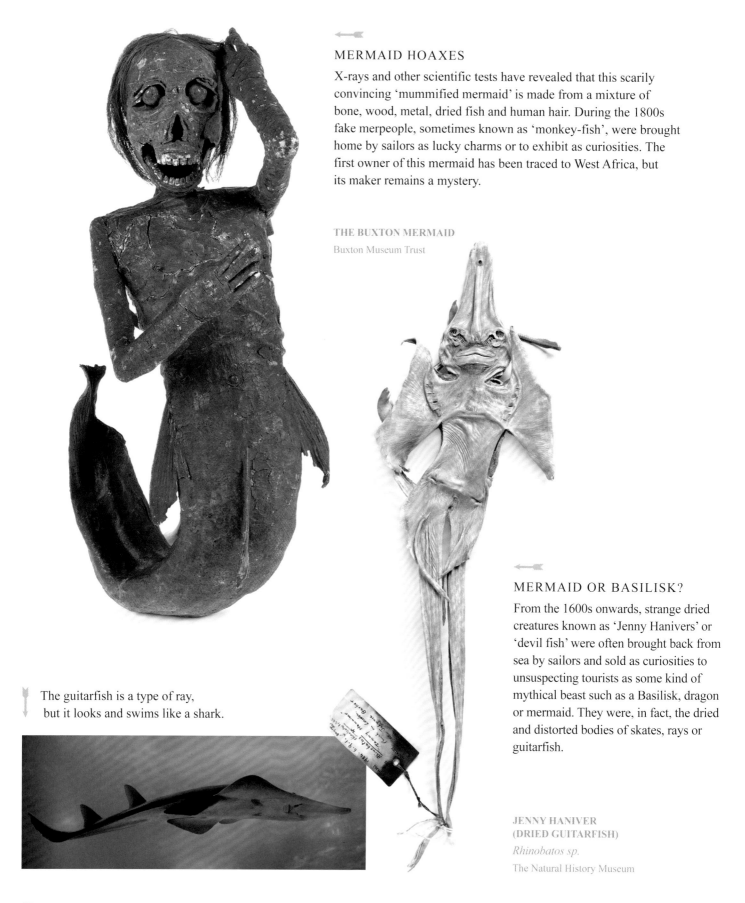

MERMAID HOAXES

X-rays and other scientific tests have revealed that this scarily convincing 'mummified mermaid' is made from a mixture of bone, wood, metal, dried fish and human hair. During the 1800s fake merpeople, sometimes known as 'monkey-fish', were brought home by sailors as lucky charms or to exhibit as curiosities. The first owner of this mermaid has been traced to West Africa, but its maker remains a mystery.

THE BUXTON MERMAID
Buxton Museum Trust

The guitarfish is a type of ray, but it looks and swims like a shark.

MERMAID OR BASILISK?

From the 1600s onwards, strange dried creatures known as 'Jenny Hanivers' or 'devil fish' were often brought back from sea by sailors and sold as curiosities to unsuspecting tourists as some kind of mythical beast such as a Basilisk, dragon or mermaid. They were, in fact, the dried and distorted bodies of skates, rays or guitarfish.

**JENNY HANIVER
(DRIED GUITARFISH)**
Rhinobatos sp.
The Natural History Museum

THE MERPEOPLE'S RIDDLE

In the first task of the Triwizard Tournament, Harry Potter wins a golden egg containing a secret riddle. When he opens it, "a loud and screechy wailing … filled the room". It is not until Harry submerges the egg in water that he can understand the mer-song that reveals the hidden message inside.

GOLDEN EGG

PROP FROM THE HARRY POTTER FILM *HARRY POTTER AND THE GOBLET OF FIRE*, 2005

Warner Bros.

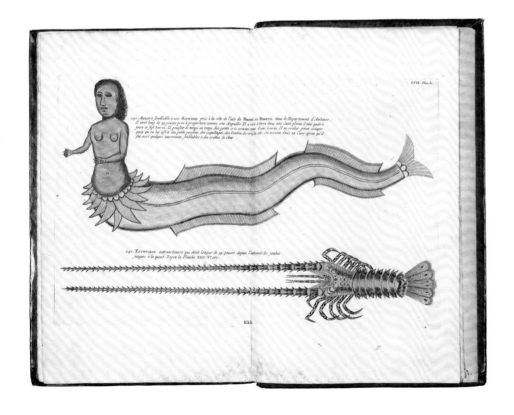

A WILD-CAUGHT MERMAID

Filled with colourful and sometimes fanciful fishes, this book by naturalist Louis Renard contains an account of "a monster resembling a Siren" caught in Indonesia. Renard describes this siren as being "59 inches long, and in proportion as an eel", and notes that "From time to time it uttered little cries like those of a mouse". He also lists several other sightings and states that the existence of mermaids is "quite definitely affirmed".

POISSONS, ECREVISSES ET CRABES (FISHES, CRAYFISH AND CRABS), 1718–1719

LOUIS RENARD, ILLUSTRATED BY SAMUEL FALLOURS

The Natural History Museum

MAGICAL HORNED BEASTS

For hundreds of years, unicorns were believed to be real animals, and people wrote about them alongside other animals in their natural history books. Tusks, bones and fossils were traded as the magical horns of these elusive, enchanting beasts. Medicines made with powdered 'unicorn horn' could be prescribed by doctors or purchased in apothecary shops to treat fevers, epilepsy or the plague. Today we know these fossilised bones belonged to prehistoric animals such as mammoths.

SIBERIAN UNICORN

Elasmotherium sibiricum (elas-mo-THEE-ree-um sie-BEER-i-kum) is an extinct species of rhinoceros. It is sometimes called the Siberian unicorn because researchers think the large bump on its skull once supported an enormous horn. By analysing fossil remains like this skull, scientists at the Natural History Museum in London have revealed that humans in Siberia, Eastern Europe and Central Asia may have lived alongside this 'unicorn' for thousands of years.

Elasmotherium sibiricum SKULL,
ABOUT 700,000–39,000 YEARS AGO,
SOUTH OF VOLGOGRAD, RUSSIA
The Natural History Museum

NARWHAL TUSK
Monodon monoceros
The Natural History Museum

SHORT HORNS AND COILED TAILS

This encyclopedia of animals was originally published in the 1650s. Among the images of horses, donkeys and zebras, the book includes several types of unicorn. Some have short horns; others have coiled tails or even webbed feet. These illustrations were based on the many different descriptions of the mythical creature written over thousands of years.

THEATRUM UNIVERSALE OMNIUM ANIMALIUM, 1718
JOANNES JONSTONUS
The Natural History Museum

Monoceros seu Unicornu aliud.

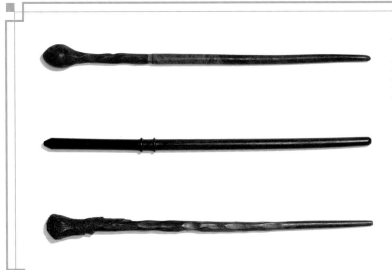

UNICORN HAIR

In the Wizarding World of J.K. Rowling, unicorn horn, hair and blood all have magical properties. Wands made with unicorn hair are faithful and produce the most consistent magic. Remus Lupin, Draco Malfoy and Ron Weasley each carry wands with a unicorn-hair core.

WANDS BELONGING TO REMUS LUPIN (TOP), DRACO MALFOY (MIDDLE) AND RON WEASLEY (BOTTOM)
PROPS FROM THE HARRY POTTER FILMS
Warner Bros.

WEAVING TALES OF UNICORNS

When this tapestry was woven around 500 years ago, many Europeans believed that unicorns were real animals. In the Late Middle Ages (around 1300–1500), artists depicted unicorns as pure white horse-like creatures with a long, twisted horn. Unicorns were said to be graceful and elusive, and their magical horns were thought to have healing powers.

MILLEFLEUR ('THOUSAND FLOWER') TAPESTRY WITH A UNICORN, ABOUT 1500
Victoria and Albert Museum

We now know that the 'unicorn horns' traded across Europe for centuries actually came from a small Arctic whale called a narwhal. Male narwhals have a single tooth (known as a tusk) emerging from the front of their heads. This tusk can grow up to 3 metres (10 feet) long. Recent studies suggest that narwhals' tusks may help the whales to find food or detect changes in sea temperature, pressure or salt content.

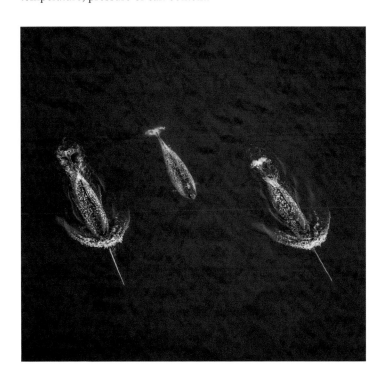

The unicorn's horn, blood and hair all have highly magical properties. It generally avoids human contact, is more likely to allow a witch to approach it than a wizard, and is so fleet of foot that it is very difficult to capture.

Fantastic Beasts and Where to Find Them

DRAWING OF A UNICORN (DRY POINT ETCHING)
OLIVIA LOMENECH GILL
Bloomsbury

MONSTERS OF THE SEA

People used to believe that huge, frightening beasts inhabited the world's oceans. Accounts of mysterious sea monsters dragging sailors and their ships to the bottom of the ocean were retold in ancient myths. Sailors came home with stories of sightings of strange creatures. But were oarfish, giant squids and other unfamiliar sea animals actually the real 'monsters' of these tall tales?

THE KRAKEN

Tales of the mythical kraken describe a gigantic octopus-like creature that attacked sailors and even entire ships. Today it is thought that sightings of giant squids and other large cephalopods (KEF-a-la-pods) such as octopuses may have inspired these stories.

HISTOIRE NATURELLE, GÉNÉRALE ET PARTICULIÈRE DES MOLLUSQUES, 1801
PIERRE DENYS DE MONTFORT
The Natural History Museum

ORIGINS OF THE KRAKEN

Encounters with giant squids are thought to be the most likely explanation for tales of sea monsters such as the kraken. These deep-sea animals are rarely seen alive, but dying squids are sometimes spotted near the water's surface or washed up on beaches. Much of what we know about giant squids has come from studying remains such as these, which were found in the stomach of a sperm whale.

HEAD AND ARMS OF A YOUNG GIANT SQUID, PARTIALLY DIGESTED
Architeuthis dux
The Natural History Museum

CLOSE ENCOUNTERS

Reports of sea serpent sightings fill this scrapbook from the 1800s. It was assembled by Richard Owen, the Natural History Museum's first superintendent, who was sceptical because no physical evidence of these monsters had ever been found. He suspected that sailors were simply misidentifying seals, whales and other marine creatures, a view that earned Owen the nickname 'Sea-Serpent Killer'.

NEWSPAPER CUTTING IN A SCRAPBOOK OF MATERIALS RELATING TO SEA SERPENTS, COLLECTED BY RICHARD OWEN, ABOUT 1830–1880s

The Natural History Museum

THE ILLUSTRATED POLICE NEWS

LAW-COURTS AND WEEKLY RECORD

SATURDAY, MAY 20, 1876.

T SEA SERPENT AS SEEN FROM THE SHIP HYDASPES

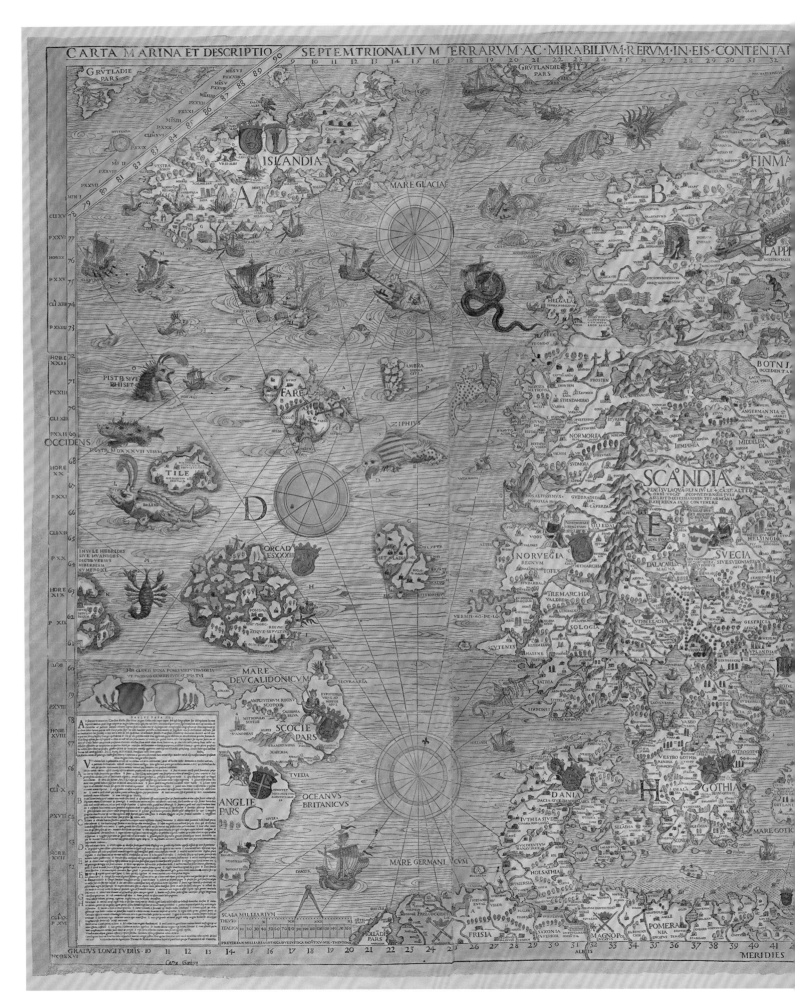

A SEA FULL OF MONSTERS

This map, drawn by Olaus Magnus, shows the seas around Scandinavia filled with ferocious creatures. Could some of these beasts actually have been real sea creatures that sailors saw and mistook for monsters? Some of them, like the terrifying red Sea Orm (pictured towards the top of the map), were the stuff of mariners' nightmares. This giant serpent was said to be over 60 metres (200 feet) long and 6 metres (20 feet) thick, and it could crush a ship to pieces with its snake-like body.

CARTA MARINA (MARINE MAP)
REPRODUCTION OF A 1949 HAND-COLOURED
FACSIMILE, 1539
OLAUS MAGNUS

The James Ford Bell Library,
University of Minnesota, USA

BONES OF A MONSTROUS FISH

These lengthy skeletal remains are those of a giant oarfish, the longest known living species of bony fish. These incredible deep-sea creatures can grow up to 8 metres (26 feet) long – over twice the length of the skeleton specimen pictured here. Scientists know little about giant oarfish behaviour because oarfish live at depths of up to 1,000 metres (3,300 feet) and are seldom encountered alive. However, rare glimpses of the silvery snake-like bodies and bright red fins of dead or dying specimens washed up on beaches are thought to be behind many of the tales of sightings of mysterious giant 'sea serpents'.

SKELETON OF A GIANT OARFISH
Regalecus glesne
The Natural History Museum

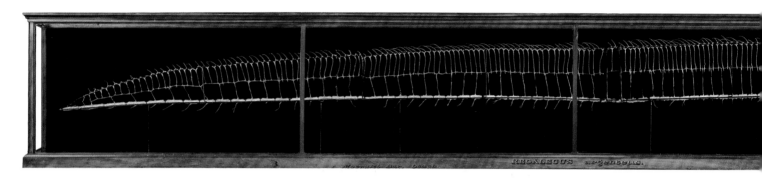

"Though alarming in appearance, sea serpents are not known ever to have killed any human, despite hysterical Muggle accounts of their ferocious behaviour."

Fantastic Beasts and Where to Find Them

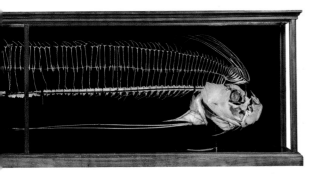

SEA SERPENT

Artist Olivia Lomenech Gill looked to the natural world for inspiration while creating artworks for an illustrated edition of *Fantastic Beasts and Where to Find Them*. Lomenech Gill writes that her etching of the sea serpent "was completely inspired by the oarfish, which I never knew about until working on this book. How fantastical that such creatures actually exist!"

PAINTING OF A SEA SERPENT (ETCHING WITH WATERCOLOUR)
OLIVIA LOMENECH GILL
Bloomsbury

A NATURAL LIFE

There have been many incredible naturalists over the years, from Pliny the Elder in ancient Roman times to Jane Goodall and others working today. The research of the early naturalists paved the way for future generations and the amazing work that these experts continue to do to protect our natural world.

Pliny the Elder, 23–79 AD

Roman author, naturalist, philosopher and naval commander in the Roman army who investigated natural, historical and geographical phenomena in the field, such as zoology, astronomy, botany, agriculture and medicine. He compiled his findings in his *Naturalis Historia* (*Natural History*), a thirty-seven volume encyclopedic work that became a model for all other encyclopedias.

Maria Sibylla Merian, 1647–1717

German-born naturalist and scientific illustrator. She was a leading entomologist of her time and one of the first naturalists to observe insects directly. Merian published several volumes of natural illustrations, in which she documented the life cycles of many different insect species. Her book *Metamorphosis Insectorum Surinamensium* (*The Metamorphosis of the Insects of Suriname*) is a detailed record of the tropical insects she studied in the region.

Carl Linnaeus, 1707–1778

Swedish physician, botanist and zoologist and father of species classification. Linnaeus proposed a hierarchical system for classifying the natural world in his published work *Systema Naturae* (*System of Nature*). His system marks the beginning of the modern scientific naming of both animals and plants into two parts – the genus (the type of organism) and the species (the specific group the organism belongs to).

> *Newton ('Newt') Artemis Fido Scamander was born in 1897. His interest in fabulous beasts was encouraged by his mother, who was an enthusiastic breeder of fancy Hippogriffs.*

Fantastic Beasts and Where to Find Them

Charles Darwin, 1809–1882

English naturalist who published his theory of evolution with fellow naturalist **Alfred Russel Wallace (1823–1913)**, who had come up with the same ideas independently. In it they claim that all species have evolved over time from common ancestors, by the process of natural selection; that being that species which can adapt to their environments will survive and continue to reproduce.

Dian Fossey, 1932–1985

American anthropologist, zoologist and primatologist. Fossey undertook an extensive eighteen year study of gorilla groups in the mountain forests of Rwanda. She lived among the gorillas, and her first-hand observations and research transformed the way in which we see and understand these incredible animals, and inspired others to continue the conservation work to protect and save them.

Jane Goodall, 1934–present

British anthropologist and primatologist. Goodall is best known for her forty-five year study of social and family interactions of wild chimpanzees in Tanzania, and is considered one of the world's leading experts on chimpanzees. She has set up an institute in her name, and runs various programmes that focus on conservation and animal welfare issues.

ME

the ... larva
a ... leaf of
...rpus Natali "
...Leigh, F.E.S.
...n (Natal) Dec: 31:
1908.

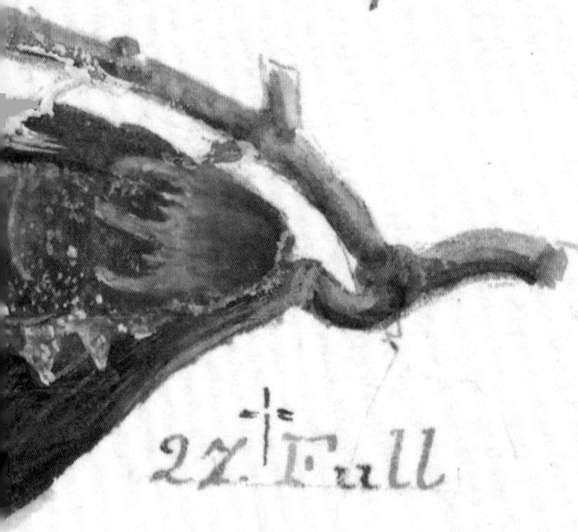

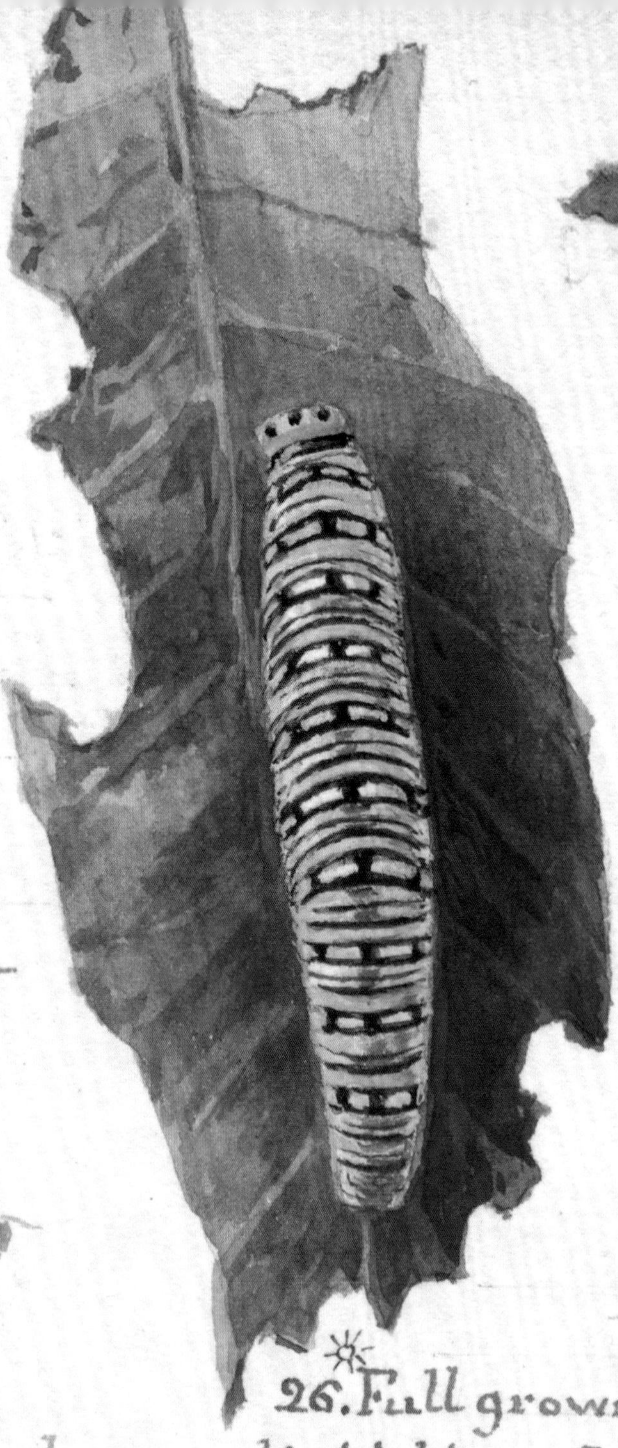

27. Full
grown
a of Charaxes
...t Chaetachme
... G.F.Leigh.
3: 1909.

26. Full grown
larva (light, tipical
form) of Hesperia
Keithloa, also on a
leaf of Acridocarpus
Natalitius. Presented
to me by Mr: G.F.Leigh.
Durban (Natal)

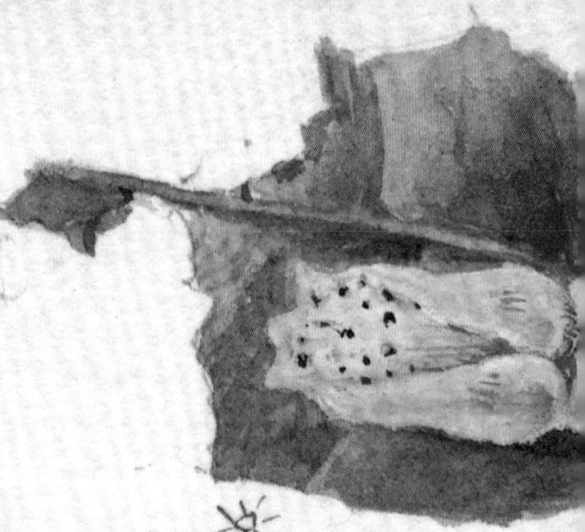

26ᵇ. Freshly ...
...of Hesperi...
Durban (Na...

26ᶜ. Pupa of
Keithloa, af...
two in the Pup...
Durba...

CHAPTER THREE

THE NATURALIST EXPLORER

*"**Fantastic Beasts and Where to Find Them** represents the fruit of many years' travel and research."*

Newt Scamander

THE NATURALIST EXPLORER

By Andrea Hart
Head of Library Special Collections, Natural History Museum

*Andrea Hart oversees one of the world's most comprehensive collections of printed
literature, artworks and manuscripts on natural history. As well as being an author
and expert advisor for Arts Council England, she also sits on the Collections
Committee at the prestigious Linnean Society of London.*

Humans have shown an interest in the natural world for thousands of years,
but it was only really during the seventeenth century that the study of nature
by careful observation and deduction came to the fore. Naturalist explorers began
to travel the globe, systematically cataloguing and analysing all that they saw,
then trying to make sense of how it worked.

At the same time in the magical world, wizards and witches were trying to
understand more about the fantastic beasts that lived among them. As early as the
fourteenth century, the wizarding community was debating the definition of 'beast',
a controversy that had been raging for centuries. Should a magical creature with
only two legs be designated a 'being' or a 'beast'? It wasn't until the nineteenth
century that a definition was found that most deemed acceptable. While a being was
agreed to be "any creature that has sufficient intelligence to understand the laws of
the magical community and to bear part of the responsibility in shaping those laws",
beasts, by default, formed a rich and diverse category ranging from Acromantula
to Zouwu. Since then Magizoologists like Newt Scamander have worked tirelessly to
further knowledge of these species, travelling the globe in search of fantastic beasts.

The early pioneers in natural history research were brave, curious and meticulous.
A particular hero of mine, Maria Sibylla Merian, was one of the first European
naturalist explorers to study insects in the field. In 1699, a time when females rarely
travelled on their own, she set off from Amsterdam to the Dutch colony of Surinam
in South America, accompanied only by her daughter, to fulfil a lifelong ambition
to document and illustrate new species of insects and the plants on which they
lived. Because the European dress style of the time was ill-suited to the climate,
she had to conduct much of her research at night, but this didn't stop her making

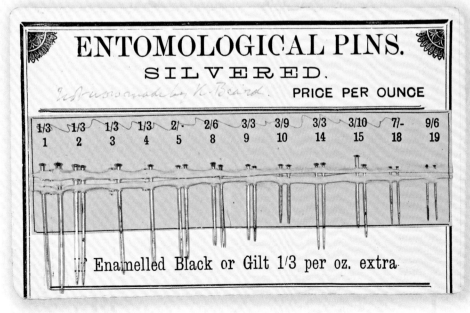

pioneering discoveries and capturing brilliantly with her paintings the life cycle of butterflies and much more. She fell ill, possibly with malaria, and was forced to return to Amsterdam after less than two years, but her *Metamorphosis Insectorum Surinamensium* was published to wide acclaim in 1705. Among the many scientists who consulted and referred to her work was Carl Linnaeus, whose system of classifying the natural world is used to this day.

Another key naturalist explorer was Alexander von Humboldt, who travelled extensively in the Americas from 1799 to 1804. Inspired by the voyages of Captain Cook and Louis-Antoine de Bougainville, he and his colleague Aimé Bonpland made the first scientific exploration of the areas that are now Venezuela, Colombia, Peru and Ecuador, and also travelled to Mexico, Cuba and the United States. They mapped much of the land as they went, and made meticulous observations and recordings throughout their travels. Between them they collected over 60,000 botanical specimens, of which 3,000 were unknown to science, and among Humboldt's many significant discoveries was what he called plant geography, which revealed that the Earth is made up of distinct regions and that where plants grow is dependent on altitude, temperature, climate and geography.

Humboldt, in turn, inspired iconic naturalist explorers such as Charles Darwin to join the five-year voyage of the HMS *Beagle* and Alfred Russel Wallace to travel first to the Amazon with his friend and fellow naturalist Henry Walter Bates and then to the Malay Archipelago. All the time they were observing and recording what they saw and trying to find explanations for things that did not make sense to them, such as the uniqueness of the animals Darwin discovered in the Galápagos Islands and the striking differences Wallace noted in the animal life on two different parts of the archipelago despite them being separated by only a narrow stretch of water. These epic journeys gave Darwin and Wallace the evidence they needed to develop groundbreaking theories on evolution by natural selection.

An expedition is rarely easy – many of the naturalist explorers faced great physical danger and mental challenges during their travels. They crossed inhospitable, strange landscapes, often at risk of catching potentially fatal diseases, the possibility of disaster never far away. Humboldt had to be saved from drowning when his canoe capsized, and Wallace lost almost everything, including his precious collections, when the ship on which he was returning from the Amazon caught fire and sank.

As we get closer to the time of Newt's travels, polar exploration added a new and exciting dimension to this field, but also brought greater danger and hardship. One of my favourite travel books is Apsley Cherry-Garrard's *The Worst Journey in the World*. On reading his commentary, you are left in no doubt that it was exactly that. Cherry-Garrard journeyed to Antarctica on Captain Scott's *Terra Nova* expedition, where they coped with incredibly challenging conditions in their determination to explore the continent in the name of science and discovery. 'The Worst Journey' saw Cherry-Garrard and his two colleagues travelling about 100 kilometres through darkness and plunging temperatures during mid-winter in a quest to collect emperor penguin eggs. It took them nineteen days to get there, enduring temperatures below −60 °C. During these extremes, Cherry-Garrard's teeth chattered so much that many of them shattered. The trip came to a fitting end when, having collected the eggs, the team nearly failed to make it back because their tent blew away during a blizzard. A naturalist's life is not for the faint-hearted!

How the naturalist explorer goes about his or her business has inevitably changed thanks to technological developments, but in some ways it has remained the same. Botanists continue to collect plants that they dry and press so they can be mounted on herbarium sheets. Entomologists still use 'pooters' to suck insects into collecting vessels and variations of the classic Victorian butterfly nets to capture flying insects. Technological advances in photography, however, have inevitably revolutionised the capturing of visual data and led to the demise of the explorer artist.

What has remained constant throughout is the importance of data. Without information listing where and when a specimen was collected, it has little use for science. Making accurate comparisons between the past and the present is only possible with accurate data, and so our historical collections, invaluably enhanced with accompanying journals and artistic visual records, are as important now as they have ever been, enabling us to understand what has changed and so predict what is likely to happen in the future.

Newt Scamander is a wonderful example of the value and importance of this practice. His carefully recorded notes, diagrams and drawings form an astonishing body of reference on how to seek out and understand the fantastic beasts of the wizarding world. His groundbreaking work even led to a ban on experimental breeding, which "effectively prevented the creation of new and untameable monsters within Britain". We owe a debt of gratitude to him and all of the great naturalist explorers of the past. Their findings and instinctive respect for nature has not only furthered our understanding today, it has opened a window on the magnificence of the world's biodiversity and ecosystems.

Andrew Hart

WHAT IS A NATURALIST?

A naturalist is a person who studies plants, animals or other living things. There are different types of naturalist – zoologists observe animals, botanists learn about plants and entomologists focus on insects. Naturalists study their subjects both out in the field and in science laboratories. They observe how plants and animals live, behave and interact with others in their natural habitats; they study breeding and feeding habits, and how living things adapt to their environments; they also analyse the impact human activities have on the survival of different species.

In the past, many European naturalists like Newt Scamander travelled to the furthest reaches of the globe to learn more about our world and the creatures we share it with. Whether driven by their passion, curiosity or commercial interests, naturalists and explorers have braved churning seas, Arctic winds and rough terrain. Their reward was to return home with tales of adventures, new discoveries and valuable scientific knowledge. The observations and collections made by naturalists in the past paved the way for the studies of scientists and conservationists today, but it is important to recognise that their work was inextricably linked with European colonialism, which had a devastating impact on local people and environments.

The research and practical fieldwork that naturalists carry out is vital for our understanding of the diversity of our natural world. Their observations show us how truly remarkable all living creatures are, and how important it is that we consider the many species that are under threat, as well as work to find solutions to safeguard them in the future.

An explorer making an expedition over land to collect plant specimens would need a sturdy pair of boots to keep their feet safe and dry, and a rucksack to carry their essential supplies like food and a first aid kit.

EXPLORERS' KIT
LEATHER BOOTS AND A CANVAS
RUCKSACK USED BY BOTANIST
NICHOLAS POLUNIN (1909–1997)
The Natural History Museum

TRAVELLING THE GLOBE

A Mappa Mundi ('map of the world') can be seen hanging inside Newt's shed in the film adaptation of *Fantastic Beasts and Where to Find Them*. While conducting research for his book, Newt encountered many magical species during his travels around the globe, from Billywigs buzzing around Australia to Thunderbirds creating storms over North America.

MAPPA MUNDI

PROP FROM THE FILM *FANTASTIC BEASTS AND WHERE TO FIND THEM*, 2016

Warner Bros.

IN THE FIELD

Most explorers aren't lucky enough to own a magical case like Newt Scamander's, which is bewitched with an Undetectable Extension Charm, allowing a multitude of creatures to live inside without an ounce of added weight. Instead they pack and carry everything they need to live and work in remote areas, such as clothes, tools, specimen bags and containers, fuel and food.

EXPLORERS' KIT ➤➤➤

Items like the ones shown here were essential for an expedition. Explorers would use a simple hook and line to help catch their dinner and to add additional fresh food to their supplies. Many Arctic explorers in the early 1900s carried tins of Bovril pemmican – a beef product high in fat and protein, with a long shelf life. And being prepared for accidents with a first aid kit is essential when you are in the wild and a long way from help.

EXPLORERS' KIT
INCLUDES A FIRST AID KIT, A FISHING LINE AND HOOK, AND A TIN OF
BOVRIL PEMMICAN
USED BY BOTANIST NICHOLAS POLUNIN (1909–1997)
The Natural History Museum

NEWT SCAMANDER

Newton Artemis Fido Scamander, known as 'Newt', is a Magizoologist – a witch or wizard who studies magical beasts. Like many explorers and naturalists, Newt Scamander has travelled the world, seeking fantastic beasts to study and observe. He has recorded his findings in his book *Fantastic Beasts and Where to Find Them*. Newt's early interest in fabulous beasts was encouraged by his mother, who was an enthusiastic breeder of fancy Hippogriffs. Newt was awarded the Order of Merlin, Second Class, in recognition of his services to the study of magical beasts.

Newt carries all the tools he needs to study and care for fantastic beasts inside a leather case. Though it seems ordinary, the case is actually a doorway into Newt's enchanted workspace, which includes a shed as well as habitats for magical creatures. Newt can hide the contents of the case from non-wizards by flicking a small switch that makes the case 'Muggle worthy'.

NEWT SCAMANDER AND HIS MAGICAL CASE
PROP FROM THE FILM *FANTASTIC BEASTS
AND WHERE TO FIND THEM*, 2016
Warner Bros.

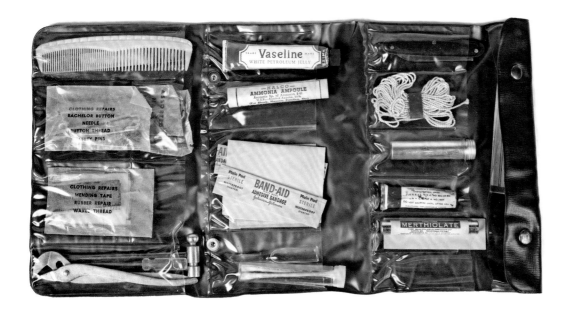

INSECT COLLECTING EQUIPMENT

Equipment like the items shown below was once used by explorers to collect and study insects. This kit includes a glass pooter to suck up small insects, a tin of treacle used to attract moths, insect pins for displaying preserved specimens, and a wooden box for breeding and observing live creatures.

INSECT COLLECTING EQUIPMENT, 1800s–1900s

INCLUDES A GLASS POOTER, A TIN OF TREACLE, INSECT PINS AND A BREEDING CAGE

FROM A COLLECTION ASSEMBLED BY ENTOMOLOGIST MICHAEL CHALMERS-HUNT (1920–2004)

The Natural History Museum

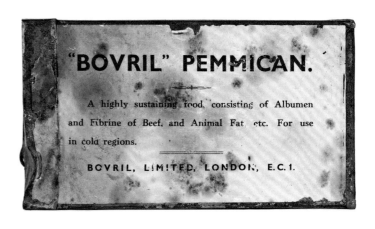

EXPLORERS' FIELD NOTES

A lot of what we know about the explorations of the early 1900s comes from the detailed drawings and notes recorded by the naturalists of that time, during their expeditions. These intrepid explorers filled the pages of their notebooks with fascinating observations about the habitats and behaviours of the creatures and plant life they encountered, and incredible sketches detailing the colours and textures of fur, feathers and skin, and flowers and vegetation.

LUCY EVELYN CHEESMAN (1881–1969)

While Magizoologist Newt Scamander was tracking fantastic beasts, entomologist Lucy Evelyn Cheesman was travelling the world studying and collecting insects. On one expedition through the rainforest of New Guinea, Cheesman drew this ink sketch. European naturalists like Cheesman often relied on the expertise and labour of local people.

EXPEDITION SKETCH, INK ON PAPER, 1930s
LUCY EVELYN CHEESMAN
The Natural History Museum

NEWT'S NOTES

Newt Scamander recorded his observations about the fantastic beasts he encountered during his travels to Burkina Faso, Seychelles, Kiribati, Laos and Chuuk, in leather-bound notebooks. A book full of blank pages for sketching and recording information is an essential item on any explorer's packing list.

NEWT'S FIELD NOTEBOOKS
PROP FROM THE FILM *FANTASTIC BEASTS AND WHERE TO FIND THEM*, 2016
Warner Bros.

The Common Sepia. Sepia Officinalis,
This & Octopus, or Squid, is the Animal
from which
the Sepia
used in Water Colour painting is procured. Also the Cuttle Fish "Bone"
from which "Prepared Chalk" is made for Tooth Powder.
The Lower
Beak

These Tentacles are
covered with
Suckers.

The Horny Upper
Beak.

OLIVIA TONGE (1858–1949)

This notebook full of paintings by Olivia Tonge records the animals and plants she encountered during her travels in India and Pakistan. She annotated her pictures with fascinating descriptions and observations.

SKETCHBOOK, WATERCOLOUR ON PAPER, 1908–1913
(ABOVE AND OVERLEAF)
OLIVIA TONGE
The Natural History Museum

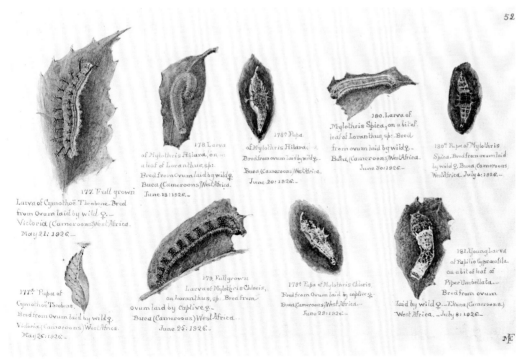

52

MARGARET FOUNTAINE (1862–1940)

This sketchbook is full of drawings that detail the life stages of butterflies, observed by the adventurous explorer Margaret Fountaine. Fountaine was a lepidopterist – a person who studies or collects butterflies and moths. She travelled around the world, collecting over 22,000 butterflies in her lifetime, and kept diaries of her journeys and expeditions.

SKETCHBOOKS OF LEPIDOPTERA,
WATERCOLOUR ON PAPER, 1931–1939
MARGARET FOUNTAINE
The Natural History Museum

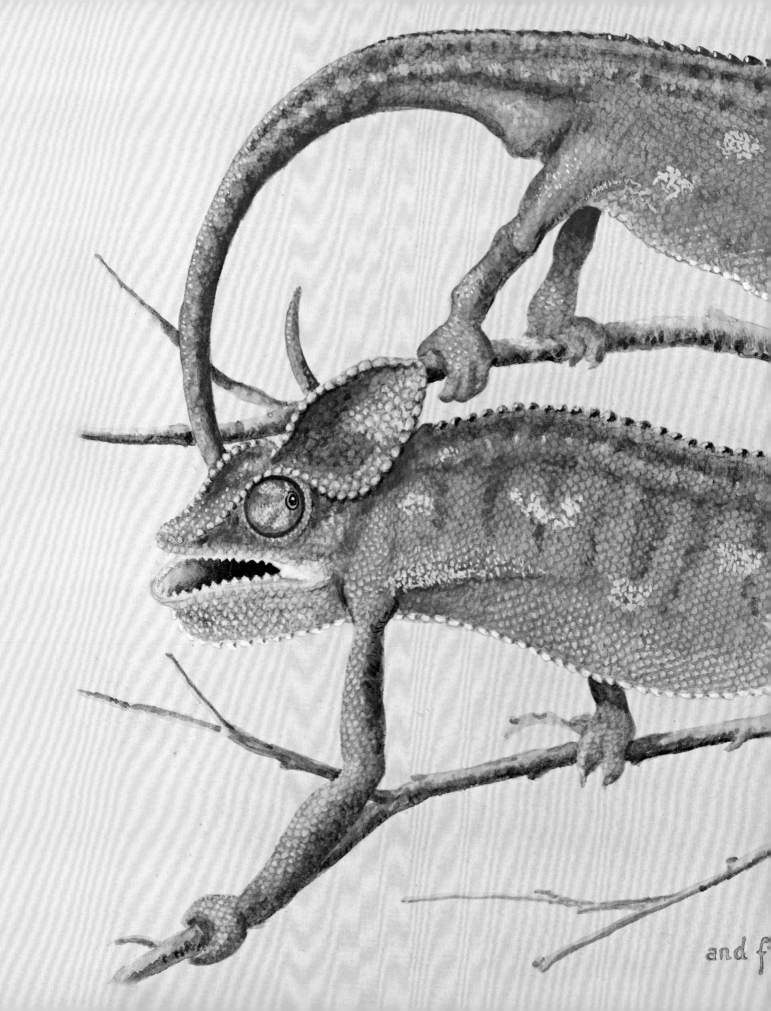

and f

The
Chameleon (Cameleo vulgaris)
which changes its Colour so wonderfully, and
Markings on its Skin from large Spots to Small,
Broad Stripes to Narrow, each Side independently.

A NATURALIST'S DIARY

By Diva Amon

Deep-sea biologist and ocean advocate

Diva is a Marie Sklodowska Curie Research Fellow at the Natural History Museum, London and co-founder of the non-profit NGO SpeSeas.

1st February 2020

We have said goodbye to dry land and are steaming out to sea on board the RRS *Discovery*. Going to sea is my favourite part of my job and I'm very much looking forward to exploring the depths of the Pacific Ocean with this team of fifty people over the next four weeks. The deep sea is *so* vast – it provides over ninety-five per cent of all habitable space and is the largest ecosystem on our planet, and I'm thrilled to be lucky enough to explore just a teeny-tiny part of it.

10th February 2020

We are only five days into our exploration but the sights have been breathtaking – an anemone-like animal with eight-foot-long tentacles that billow across the sea floor, foot-long purple sea cucumbers with sails to help them swim, red and yellow jellyfish … some of these species never seen before by human eyes. There are very few careers that allow you to be among the first people on the planet to see a species or habitat or behaviour!

Less than one per cent of the deep ocean has been seen by cameras or by human eyes. And on this expedition, despite nearly a month spent surveying using a suite of tools that includes trawl nets, box cores, baited cameras and traps, remotely operated vehicles (ROVs), and autonomous underwater vehicles, we will just scratch the surface in understanding what lives here. Speaking of which, the ROV is just about to go in the water so I need to head to the control van. More later!

11th February 2020

I am exhausted after surveying the deep-sea floor for twelve hours using the ROV. It's now on its way back to the surface laden with rock and animal samples to be processed. Meticulously taking specimen photos, measurements and tissue samples for DNA is time consuming, but once these animals are preserved in ethanol or formaldehyde, they won't ever look the same so it is important to catalogue them as precisely as possible before packaging them up to be shipped back to the lab at the Natural History Museum in London, where we will study them in much greater detail.

18th February 2020

The ROV dive today was sobering. We saw six pieces of human refuse – two plastic bags, one plastic bottle, a glass bottle, a metal paint tin and a piece of fishing line. This has happened on every research cruise that I have been on. And these are just the human impacts that we can see – what about chemical pollution, microplastics or climate change? Sadly, even if we have never been there, evidence of us has – there is no place on this planet that can escape our touch.

10th March 2020

The team plus three crate-loads of samples have made it safely to the Deep-Sea Lab at the Natural History Museum in London. We will spend the next year looking at each animal's morphology and examining their DNA. This will allow us to ascertain whether these species are known or new to science. If they are new, we will then have to describe them and give them names. If they are known, we will begin to get a better picture of where in the world's oceans they live.

This research is the first step in understanding what lives in a tiny part of the Pacific Ocean, as well as learning more about the ecology of these animals, such as what they eat, how they reproduce and what role they play in the deep ocean. We are cataloguing the life on this incredible planet, and this baseline understanding is crucial to being able to understand how the deep sea is changing.

CHAPTER FOUR

HIDDEN CREATURES

"Perhaps the most important step in the concealment of magical creatures is the creation of safe habitats."

Newt Scamander

HIDDEN CREATURES

By Olivia Lomenech Gill
Printmaker, illustrator and fine artist

*Olivia Lomenech Gill is the visionary artist behind the stunning Illustrated Edition of J.K. Rowling's **Fantastic Beasts and Where to Find Them**. Her work is alive with creatures – both real and imagined – rendered in a dazzling array of techniques.*

When I was asked to illustrate J.K. Rowling's *Fantastic Beasts and Where to Find Them*, it was a unique proposition. It is probably always difficult, impossible even, for an artist to clearly describe their creative process, especially as, working on an illustration commission, one is obliged to adapt to and enter into the world of the writer using the text they have created. Every entry in Newt Scamander's alphabetical reference book is succinct, minimal even. I remember quite early on realising (maybe with some relief!) that in fact this work, being a 'library' book, stands alone from the Harry Potter narrative and that the beasts described within are archetypes. This realisation allowed me to approach it as a dictionary or, rather, a bestiary. That was my way in.

So how would I begin to make these magical species appear on the page? The project was a particularly interesting challenge for me because I am a very literal artist. This means that I work from real-life inspiration and observation. It was my literal approach that dictated how I went about creating the illustrations for *Fantastic Beasts*.

My starting point was to book a session in the reading room at the Natural History Museum to look at original copies of Ulisse Aldrovandi's *Monstrorum Historia* and Conrad Gessner's *Historia Animalium*, two of the best-known Renaissance zoological reference books. Written in the sixteenth century, these enormous tomes are extraordinary in every respect – the lack of discrimination between real and imaginary species, the layout and orientation of the illustrations, the most famous of which, Dürer's *Rhinoceros*, I was amazed to find upended, sitting on its bottom, in order to fit the page layout!

I am fascinated by old books and as a printmaker I am particularly in awe of the skill of the engravers who produced the illustrations. My husband is a paper

restorer and so there are often samples of antiquarian books, maps and other things lying around in the back of the workshop where I have my printing press. As a largely self-taught artist, I use a variety of techniques, often in combination. This includes the traditional technique of etching, usually on copper plate, using an acid or alkali solution to 'bite' the drawn image into the metal plate. It involves a combination of chemistry and serendipity. I use a three-ton printing press to produce quite a lot of my work, and probably about a third of the art in *Fantastic Beasts* involves etching or drypoint to some degree.

Of course the amazing collections of the Natural History Museum and other museums are a great source of inspiration to so many people, and they are an especially valuable resource for artists. Every time I embark on a new body of work or project I am overwhelmed by how much I don't know, particularly in relation to the natural world. By really looking and observing, I try to learn about a subject in my own way. Having the opportunity to study an array of real beasts was hugely exciting.

Quite early on in the project I worked out that there were three categories of beast – some were classic mythological creatures, such as the Chimaera; some, such as the Erumpent and the Chizpurfle, were actually (and delightfully) based on real fantastic beasts in that they are described as resembling species of the real world; and then there are some creatures that are born entirely out of J.K. Rowling's imagination, such as the Puffskein, the Fwooper and the Flobberworm.

I got into the habit of looking up the name of each new entry to see if it correlated with something real. Sometimes I struck lucky – when I typed in Ramora, as per the magical aquatic guardian of seafarers, I found the real-life remora. Often known as the 'sharksucker fish', people may be accustomed to seeing it on wildlife documentaries attached to larger fish as part of a symbiotic relationship. So I drew one of these and then, in the style of eighteenth- and nineteenth-century natural history illustration, created a cross-section detail and a landscape scene on the same page. This was a good opportunity to practice my cross-hatching!

Wherever possible I sought out real species to draw from. The Graphorn was composed of part giant ground sloth and part *Triceratops*. I visited the Naturalis collection at Leiden University in the Netherlands, as well as the more local Great North Museum: Hancock and the Gunther von Hagens *Animals Inside Out* exhibition at the Life Science Centre in Newcastle. It might sound morbid to study corpses of any description, but that is how artists have been learning anatomy since the Renaissance and before. Another great source of inspiration was the Kielder Water Birds of Prey Centre in Northumberland. There I was able to draw a live American black vulture for the Augurey, a Steller's sea eagle for the Hippogriff and a white-tailed eagle for the griffin. Birds of prey in particular move all the time, so being able to gain close proximity to such incredible creatures was a hugely valuable experience.

For my dragon illustrations, I looked at bird and bat wings and the aerodynamic possibilities of a very large beast being able to carry itself through the air. Dragons are often depicted with small wings, but I wanted to make flight for the ten dragons in *Fantastic Beasts* a little more feasible. I am not sure if I achieved this or not, but the Ukrainian Ironbelly, which was given fold-out pages, does have big wings. Being able to add a seascape or other landscape contexts to some of the beasts helped to give them a scale and a context. And of course, I looked at lizards too, although I haven't to date found any with wings …

The phoenix, as my eldest son (much to my disappointment) immediately identified, was inspired by the snake-hunting secretary bird. I chose this as my inspiration long before I became aware that Fawkes, the phoenix in the Harry Potter stories, blinds the Basilisk, a giant serpent. I don't know whether I was magically drawn to this connection, or whether it was just coincidental, but it felt serendipitous. The phoenix infant, reborn from the ashes, was sketched from a barn owl chick at Kielder. How can a whole barn owl, in all of its magnificence, invested with at least 20,000 feathers, emerge from a single egg? And how can such a majestic bird start out looking so grotesque and vulnerable? It is these sorts of things that I find truly fantastic. All of this observation and reflection fed into the illustrations for the book.

Gradually, creature by creature, my Illustrated Edition was born. All of the things that I had learned, all of the animals that I had seen, were poured into its pages. Of course I would have loved to have travelled around the world, like Newt, to study these creatures in their habitats, but I dislike flying with a vengeance. Instead I was obliged to partake in virtual voyaging, in which respect the internet is a useful tool. But more importantly, I came to question the notion of exoticism and fantasy. "A wise man marvels at the commonplace", as Confucius is supposed to have said, yet this is easily forgotten in an age where people seem to be on the move all the time and overwhelmed with information. In looking about us, it may be that we discover things we never knew were there, and that is a real form of magic! I found the toad that sits on the Basilisk's egg under my studio; the model for the Chizpurfle, a brown crab, came from the North Sea; and I discovered a Dugbog in the marsh up the road from my house. As each species emerged, living and breathing, I was overwhelmed by the magic of the wildlife that surrounds us. Nature is endlessly captivating, in all of its fantastic forms.

ANIMAL ADAPTATION

Like the fantastic beasts of the wizarding world, which can vanish at will or keep themselves cleverly out of sight, many real-life animals have evolved and adapted very specifically to the environments they live in. These species are able to use their highly developed senses to detect danger, or the patterns and colours of their skin to 'disappear' into their surroundings, allowing them to stay hidden from their predators or to silently creep up on their prey.

Adaptation to an environment, whether it is through staying cleverly hidden away or by mimicking that habitat with camouflage, can make the difference between life and death. Unlike most animals, cephalopods such as octopuses, squid and cuttlefish are capable of dramatically and quickly changing the colour and texture of their skin, or even their entire body shape, to 'vanish' into their underwater world. More commonly, animals evolve with a camouflaged skin pattern or colour that blends in with their environment. The patterns and stripes on the fur of big cats like the jaguar and the tiger break up the shape of their bodies so that they merge with the grass and leaves they are prowling in. Insects can be masters of disguise, too – thousands of species have evolved to look like the leaves, bark and sticks they live among. And elusive creatures like the okapi or the Canada lynx use their sharp senses to alert them to approaching threats, and keep themselves hidden away using the cover of their forest habitats to forage or hunt. Some species are even more challenging to observe. The rarely seen Mexican burrowing toad, for example, only comes out of its underground burrow to breed.

Unfortunately human activities such as deforestation are threatening the carefully balanced environments of many animals. If their forest home is destroyed, then there is nowhere for the creatures that live there to hide. Scientists in the field are now using high-tech equipment and DNA testing to track and monitor vulnerable species so that they can protect their homes and environments and prevent these incredible creatures from vanishing altogether.

The jaguar's (*Panthera onca*) fur is covered in dark, rose-shaped markings called rosettes. These markings disrupt the outline of the jaguar's body, making it harder to see it in its natural habitat of the forests and grasslands of Central and South America. Researchers have found that markings like these evolved specifically in large cats that tend to hunt in forests or at night.

"*Luckily, some species do not require much wizarding assistance in avoiding the notice of Muggles. Creatures such as the Tebo, the Demiguise and the Bowtruckle have their own highly effective means of camouflage and no intervention by the Ministry of Magic has ever been necessary on their behalf.*"

Fantastic Beasts and Where to Find Them

VANISHING ACTS

I t is difficult to be completely invisible without magic, but many animals have evolved equally remarkable ways of 'disappearing' to help them survive. From colour-changing chameleons and cuttlefish to patterned jaguars, algae-covered sloths, butterflies masquerading as leaves, and insects that look like sticks, these amazing creatures are true masters of disguise.

ALGAE DISGUISE ⟫

Hanging from branches high overhead, the sloth's slow movement and brown fur help it stay hidden from predators such as harpy eagles. During the rainy season, microscopic plant-like organisms (*Trichophilus* spp.) grow on the sloth's wet fur. Some scientists suspect this coating of green algae may make sloths even harder to spot among the treetops of the tropical rainforests of their South American native home.

PALE-THROATED SLOTH
Bradypus tridactylus
The Natural History Museum

A few species of green algae have been found growing on the fur of sloths. Scientists think that these microscopic plant-like organisms may be passed from mother sloths to their young.

> *The Demiguise is found in the Far East, though only with great difficulty, for this beast is able to make itself invisible when threatened and can be seen only by wizards skilled in its capture.*

Fantastic Beasts and Where to Find Them

DEMIGUISE

In the wizarding world, the Demiguise is able to make itself invisible when threatened. This magical creature has become vulnerable because its long, silky, silvery hair can be spun into Invisibility Cloaks, making Demiguise pelts highly valued.

In our world, many animals, such as tigers and jaguars, are still hunted and killed for their fur. Conservationists are working hard to stop this brutal and unnecessary trade. These animals cannot become completely invisible like the Demiguise. The patterns and colours of their fur, which help to camouflage them in the wild, is sadly also the reason they are hunted.

DOUGAL THE DEMIGUISE

FROM THE FILM *FANTASTIC BEASTS AND WHERE TO FIND THEM*, 2016
Warner Bros.

COLOUR CHANGER

Chameleons are famed for their colour-changing abilities. However, when it comes to camouflage, chameleons only make small adjustments to the shade of their generally green or brown skin. Research shows that the bursts of red, orange and yellow seen in some chameleons are used to attract mates or scare off rivals rather than to help them hide from predators.

COMMON CHAMELEON
Chamaeleo chamaeleon
The Natural History Museum

Chameleons' skin contains cells called iridophores (i-RID-ah-fors). Inside these cells are tiny crystals that reflect light and produce different colours as they move closer together or further apart.

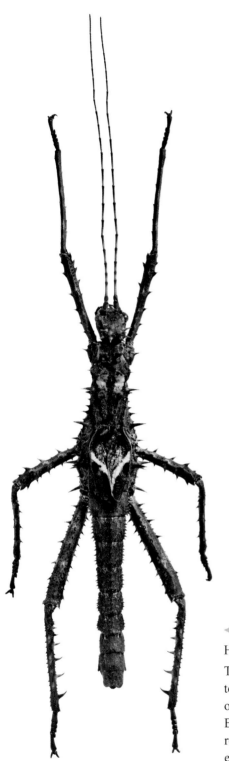

HARD TO FIND

Thousands of insect species have evolved to take the shape, colour, and even texture of the sticks and leaves they live among. By day, stick and leaf insects generally remain as still as possible to avoid being eaten by birds. Some even rock back and forth to mimic the movement of swaying branches and leaves.

STICK INSECT
Phasmida
The Natural History Museum

LEAF OR BUTTERFLY?

With its dull brown, veiny pattern, this butterfly has a remarkable form of disguise. It has evolved to look like a shrivelled dry leaf. By simply closing its wings to hide its bright colourings, the dead leaf butterfly can hide in plain sight in the forests of Eastern and Southern Asia, where it lives.

DEAD LEAF BUTTERFLY
Kallima inachus
The Natural History Museum

A master of disguise, the mimic octopus (*Thaumoctopus mimicus*) was first discovered in 1998. Like many other cephalopods, it is able to change the texture and colour of its skin to blend into its surroundings when threatened. Unusually, it has also been observed mimicking the behaviour of other more dangerous creatures in order to scare off predators.

A cuttlefish (*Sepia officinalis*) can change the colour and texture of its skin to look like a craggy coral or a sandy sea floor in under a second. Cuttlefish, as well as octopuses and squid, have soft bodies that make them vulnerable. Many species have evolved the ability to camouflage themselves by changing their appearance. This helps them to hunt, and to escape the attention of ocean predators.

This shrimp-like animal (*Cystisoma* sp.) called an amphipod (AM-fi-pod) lives in the deep ocean, where there is nowhere to hide. Apart from its eyes and egg pouch, its body is entirely transparent, making it almost invisible. Scientists have recently discovered that its body is covered in tiny bumps that help prevent light from bouncing off the surface. This makes it even more difficult to see.

ELUSIVE CREATURES

Many animals are difficult to spot in the wild. Like the Mooncalf of the wizarding world, some animals can only be seen above ground at certain times of the year. Others rely on their sharp senses of vision, hearing and smell to be able to sneak up on their prey or to escape the notice of their predators. These adaptations also help them avoid humans. To catch a glimpse of these rarely seen creatures, you need to know when, where and how to look for them.

" Then there are those beasts that, due to cleverness or innate shyness, avoid contact with Muggles at all costs — for instance, the unicorn, the Mooncalf and the centaur. "

Fantastic Beasts and Where to Find Them

STRIKING MARKINGS ➤

In 1900, British explorer Harry Johnston set out to find a "strange horse-like animal of striking markings in black and white" said to live in the forests of Central Africa. This animal was well known to the local people, who told Johnston it was called an 'o'api', or 'okapi'. Though unable to catch a glimpse of the creature, Johnston obtained a belt, pictured here, which became the first scientific record of the okapi.

BELT MADE FROM OKAPI SKIN
Okapia johnstoni
The Natural History Museum

RARELY SEEN

This shy animal is well-adapted to avoiding predators, including leopards and humans. The okapis' zebra-like markings help camouflage them among the dense, shadowy forests of the Democratic Republic of the Congo, where they live, while their sharp hearing keeps them alert to approaching threats. Okapi have long been known to local people, but European scientists did not know they existed until the early 1900s. Observing okapi in the wild remains a challenge, even today.

OKAPI
Okapia johnstoni
The Natural History Museum

Researchers leave camera traps in the forest to observe okapis without disturbing them. The okapi is an endangered species that faces threats from deforestation, poaching and other human activities. No one knows exactly how many okapis remain in the wild, but information from camera traps helps researchers estimate their population size. Researchers can also identify individual okapis based on their unique stripe patterns.

MOONCALF

"The Mooncalf is an intensely shy creature that emerges from its burrow only at the full moon. Its body is smooth and pale grey, it has bulging round eyes on top of its head and four spindly legs with enormous flat feet. Mooncalves perform complicated dances on their hind legs in isolated areas in the moonlight. These are believed to be a prelude to mating (and often leave intricate geometric patterns behind in wheat fields, to the great puzzlement of Muggles).

Watching Mooncalves dance by moonlight is a fascinating experience and often profitable, for if their silvery dung is collected before the sun rises and spread upon magical herb and flower beds, the plants will grow very fast and become extremely strong. Mooncalves are found worldwide."

Fantastic Beasts and Where to Find Them

Like the magical Mooncalf, the mysterious Mexican burrowing toad (*Rhinophrynus dorsalis*) spends most of its time hidden in its underground burrow. Scientists suspect that it emerges above ground only once a year when it comes out to breed after heavy rainstorms. Researchers looking for this elusive creature find it by following the sound of its loud, wailing mating call.

Recognisable by their tufted ears, Canada lynx (*Lynx canadensis*) rely on their sharp hearing and vision to find snowshoe hares (*Lepus americanus*), their main prey. Well-adapted to cold northern forests, these secretive, solitary hunters are rarely encountered by people. The lynx's wide, padded paws help them walk over deep powdery snow as they silently stalk their next meal.

LUNASCOPE

A Lunascope is a magical tool that helps wizards identify phases of the Moon. Newt Scamander carries a Lunascope with him to New York in *Fantastic Beasts and Where to Find Them*. In his book, Newt describes a creature – the elusive Mooncalf – that can only be seen during a full moon.

LUNASCOPE

PROP FROM THE FILM *FANTASTIC BEASTS AND WHERE TO FIND THEM*, 2016

Warner Bros.

CHAPTER FIVE

CURIOUS BEHAVIOUR

"I have visited lairs, burrows and nests across five continents, observed the curious habits of magical beasts in a hundred countries ..."

Newt Scamander

CURIOUS BEHAVIOUR

By Dr Helen Pilcher

Science writer, presenter and comedian

*Helen Pilcher is a tea-drinking, biscuit-nibbling science and comedy writer. She is scientific advisor to the **Beano**, owns a genetically modified wolf, and is the world's biggest kākāpō fan. Her most recent book, **Life Changing: How Humans are Altering Life on Earth**, features chihuahuas, golden gnus and spider-goats.*

Here's a question for any budding Magizoologists out there. What shrieks like a demonic guinea pig, 'chings' like an old-fashioned cash register and 'booms' like the bassline of a house music anthem? Need a few more clues? It has wings, but it can't fly. It smells like the inside of an old violin case. Its beady eyes are framed by flamboyant saucers of soft yellow quills, making it look like a feathery Elton John. It is one of the most curious creatures on the planet and if Newt were lucky enough to see one, he'd almost certainly want to stash it in his leather case and take care of it forever.

Still no idea? Then let me introduce you to the kākāpō – one of the most fantastic beasts I know. Critically endangered, this chunky, ground-dwelling parrot lives on a handful of islands scattered off the coast of New Zealand. Its behaviour is bizarre to say the least. Thirty years ago, when author Douglas Adams went to visit the islands, he claimed not just that the birds had forgotten how to fly, but that they had *forgotten* they had forgotten how to fly. When spooked, an anxious kākāpō will run up a tree and then fling itself to the ground with all the grace of a concrete block. It's also the only parrot to operate a 'lek breeding system', which means that males compete with each other to sing the sexiest song. They build special platforms called 'bowls', waddle into the centre of the stage, and then boom all night, every night, for months at a time. The winner gets to mate. It's like *The X Factor*, but for birds.

Scientists go to great lengths to study and protect this unusual species, but it's not easy. For starters, as of 2020 there are only around 210 kākāpō alive, making them rarer than a Golden Snidget. In addition, their mossy, mottled feathers help them to blend in with the islands' thick green foliage. That's why, in order to help keep track of the species, naturalists have fitted all of the adult kākāpō with

backpacks containing radio transmitters. The bijou accessory fits snuggly around their wings and each transmitter emits its own unique signal. Armed with a special receiver, scientists can now monitor and identify every single bird. Not just that, the transmitters also eavesdrop on any nocturnal shenanigans that might occur. The electronic devices reveal not just which birds have mated, they also give the encounter a score. Talk about pressure to perform!

Backpacks like this are just one of the ways that scientists monitor the behaviour of wild animals, but the approach isn't suitable for all species. I can't, for example, imagine a fantastic beast like a Murtlap sitting patiently while the lightweight luggage is slipped over its tentacles. Imagine, however, what Newt could achieve if he had access to twenty-first century conservation technology.

Under the ocean, for example, remotely operated vehicles (ROVs) are shining a light on the curious behaviour of another creature – the octopus *Graneledone boreopacifica*. Researchers already know that octopuses can be devoted mothers, but they had no idea how devoted until they spotted a ghostly, solitary female clinging to the side of a deep underwater canyon off the coast of California, USA. Illuminated by the ROV's headlamps, they could see that the mother was cradling around a hundred eggs, so they sent the ROV down regularly to check on her. On each occasion, the mother was found in exactly the same place, brooding her young. In the months and years that followed, she neither ate nor moved as her youngsters developed inside their egg cases. Then, on the ROV's eighteenth visit, the scientists discovered that the egg cases were empty and the mother had gone. Exhausted mother octopuses often die when their eggs hatch, but this individual had set a new record. Before she expired, the mother had brooded her young for a staggering four and a half years – by far the longest egg-brooding period ever recorded for any animal species. She gave the ultimate sacrifice so her youngsters could set out with the best possible start in life.

Above ground, camera traps are another recent technology widely used to study the behaviour of wildlife. Placed in the field for months at a time, camera traps enable scientists to spot elusive and rare species. In 2019, they were used to confirm the existence of a small, deer-like mammal dwelling in a Vietnamese forest – the silver-backed chevrotain. It was the first time the animal had been spotted in thirty years. Perhaps the same technology could help Newt locate the Diricawl, a frustratingly evasive bird? The magical creature has the capacity to disappear when it feels threatened, and then reappear in an entirely different area. It's certainly an interesting idea.

Thermal video cameras might come in handy to a busy Magizoologist in the field – they enable scientists to study visible animals, like the tiger, in the dark, and invisible animals, such as the Demiguise, at any time. If Dougal the Demiguise were to wander in front of a thermal camera, his body heat would instantly give him away.

Drones could also be put to good use. Loaded with the latest cameras, they can be primed to track animals through just about any habitat, including deserts, jungles and oceans. The technology is now so advanced that scientists can sometimes even use drones to identify specific individuals. Perhaps they could help Newt locate any missing Erumpents he might be seeking?

If all else fails, Newt could turn to one other modern method. As animals go about their everyday business they shed droppings, urine, eggs, sperm, skin cells and hair into the world around them. These biological substances contain tiny amounts of the animal's DNA, which can then become incorporated into the environment. The genetic material is called environmental DNA, or 'eDNA' for short. Scientists go out into the wild to collect samples of soil, water, ice and even snow, and then analyse the DNA that has been deposited there. By comparing their findings against a database of known DNA sequences, they can then determine the creature's identity. In 2019, eDNA collected from remote Australian waterholes was used to detect the presence of an endangered bird called the Gouldian finch. Scientists weren't able to observe the bright little bird itself, but they could infer its presence from the DNA it left behind. Meanwhile, in Scotland, the same technique has been used to probe the deep, dark waters of Loch Ness for signs of the legendary monster. So far scientists have drawn a blank, but they would do well to keep trying. According to Newt, the Loch Ness Monster is in fact a kelpie, a shape-shifting water demon. Perhaps there is eDNA out there still to be found?

The world, it seems, is always ready to surprise us with even more wondrous creatures. As we study these spectacular species, science is there to help anyone who wants to learn more about their endlessly inventive behaviour and amazing ways.

Helen Pilcher

AMAZING INTERACTIONS

From nature's most extraordinary dancers to those that can change their shape and size, our world contains an incredible diversity of creatures to discover and admire. Some animals team up with an unusual companion to work together for their mutual benefit. Others gather materials to build or protect their homes, to make food stores or to impress a potential mate. It is the same in the wizarding world. The tiny magical Bowtruckle will attack to defend the tree it lives in, and the enormous Erumpent dances to attract a mate.

Take a look at the relationship between these two unusual partners – pistol shrimps and fish known as shrimp gobies. Pistol shrimps are great at digging burrows, but their poor eyesight means that they struggle to spot danger. Fortunately, their excellent housekeeping attracts a helpful companion. Shrimp gobies enjoy the safety of pistol shrimps' burrows and look out for danger when the species venture outside.

Fascinating behaviour can be found all over the planet. In the forests of Southeast China, the female bone-house wasp collects dead ants, which it uses to disguise its nest. In Australia, the male peacock spider performs a remarkable dance to attract a female mating partner, the bright metallic-coloured patterns on its abdomen shimmering as it hops about and lifts up its legs. And there are some incredible creatures that change shape to protect themselves, such as the porcupinefish, which can puff its body up to make itself look more menacing.

By observing these behaviours, scientists have a better understanding of how different animals collaborate with other species to safeguard their mutual survival, put on elaborate dance displays to ensure they find a mate, or use their own body's defence mechanisms to protect themselves.

"I offer this work as a mere introduction to the wealth of fantastic beasts that inhabit our world."

Fantastic Beasts and Where to Find Them

SHAPE CHANGER

The spot-fin porcupinefish inflates its body by pumping water into its stomach, stretching its skin and forcing its spines upright, making it a much less appealing meal for any predator.

SPOT-FIN PORCUPINEFISH (INFLATED AND NORMAL SIZE)
Diodon hystrix
The Natural History Museum

Pistol shrimps keep one antenna (a 'feeler') touching their shrimp goby companions. If the fish senses a threat and suddenly darts back inside the shrimp's burrow, the shrimp knows to quickly follow to escape the danger.

SMELLY NEST

As you might guess from its name, the bone-house wasp collects something gruesome. The female gathers dead ants to seal the end of its nesting hole. Scientists think the corpses make the nest smell like an ant colony, which has the effect of deterring predators.

BONE-HOUSE WASP
Deuteragenia ossarium
The Natural History Museum

TEAMING UP FOR SAFETY

The magical Bowtruckles of the wizarding world protect the trees they live on and gain a safe home in return. Like them, many animals and plants have relationships where they both benefit from cooperating or living together. This is called 'mutualism'. Sometimes one animal will provide protection, often in exchange for food or shelter. Animals and plants that collaborate in this way have evolved to stay safe from predators thanks to their unusual companions.

Whistling thorn acacia trees (*Vachellia drepanolobium*) protect themselves with hundreds of sharp spines. The base of these spines also provides a home for ants. These ants (*Crematogaster mimosae*) fiercely defend the tree from anything trying to eat its leaves. Scientists have shown that the ants' bites and venom can even fend off giraffes and elephants. Giraffe calves are particularly sensitive to ant attacks, though older giraffes are less affected.

PICKETT'S PORTABLE HOME

Newt cares for several Bowtruckles, one of which, named Pickett, he often carries around in his jacket pocket. Newt keeps a small cutting of a Bowtruckle tree on his desk so that Pickett has somewhere to rest while Newt is working.

BOWTRUCKLE TREE CUTTING
PROP FROM THE FILM *FANTASTIC BEASTS: THE CRIMES OF GRINDELWALD*, 2018
Warner Bros.

Many large African herbivores, like elephants and giraffes, are under serious threat and their populations are declining fast. This could have unexpected effects on the wider ecosystems that they are part of. Research shows that when there are no herbivores grazing on the whistling thorn acacia, the tree stops producing its spiny homes for its ant bodyguards. As this relationship breaks down, the ants are often replaced by another species that can instead damage the tree, causing slower growth and higher death rates.

BOWTRUCKLE

" The Bowtruckle is a tree-guardian creature found mainly in the west of England, southern Germany and certain Scandinavian forests. It is immensely difficult to spot, being small (maximum eight inches in height) and apparently made of bark and twigs with two small brown eyes.

The Bowtruckle, which eats insects, is a peaceable and intensely shy creature but if the tree in which it lives is threatened, it has been known to leap down upon the woodcutter or tree-surgeon attempting to harm its home and gouge at their eyes with its long, sharp fingers. An offering of woodlice will placate the Bowtruckle long enough to let a witch or wizard remove wand-wood from its tree. "

Fantastic Beasts and Where to Find Them

Red-billed oxpeckers (*Buphagus erythrorhychus*) feed on the parasites of large grazing animals such as rhinoceroses. While the bird gets a good meal, its host benefits from the removal of blood-sucking ticks. The oxpecker also acts as an alarm. If it spots a predator approaching, it flies off making a shrill alarm call that rhinos and other animals have learned to respond to. Unfortunately, oxpecker alarm calls cannot protect their host from poachers. Between 1970 and 1992, black rhinoceros (*Diceros bicornis*) populations decreased by ninety-six per cent, due mainly to illegal hunting for their horns.

Newt's Bowtruckle companion, Pickett, can pick locks. This handy ability sometimes helps Newt escape from dangerous situations.

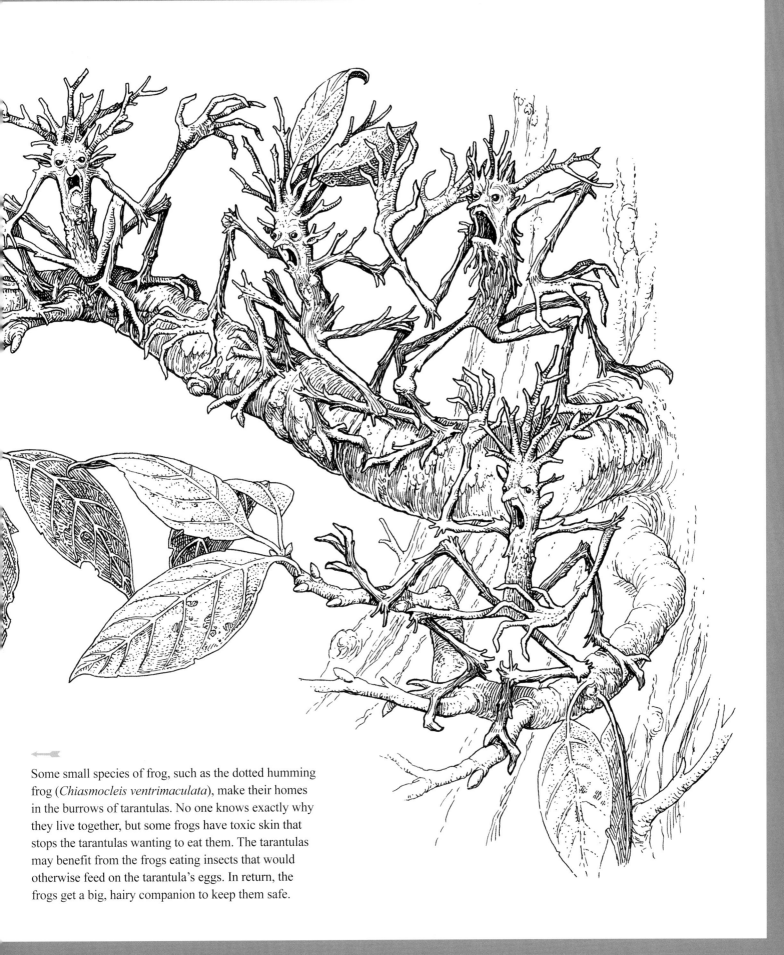

Some small species of frog, such as the dotted humming frog (*Chiasmocleis ventrimaculata*), make their homes in the burrows of tarantulas. No one knows exactly why they live together, but some frogs have toxic skin that stops the tarantulas wanting to eat them. The tarantulas may benefit from the frogs eating insects that would otherwise feed on the tarantula's eggs. In return, the frogs get a big, hairy companion to keep them safe.

CURIOUS COLLECTORS

Like the wizarding world's fluffy Niffler, many different animals collect things for all sorts of reasons. Some gather materials to build a nest or home, or to store food for the future. Others create displays of colourful items they have found to impress a potential mate.

TREASURE TROVE ⟹

Feathers, flowers, shells and even buttons and bottle tops feature in this bird's treasure trove. To attract a mate, a male satin bowerbird (pictured, top) gathers colourful objects to decorate its bower, a tunnel-like structure made from sticks. When a female appears, the male performs a dance while holding a favourite object in its beak.

MALE AND FEMALE SATIN BOWERBIRDS
Ptilonorhynchus violaceus
The Natural History Museum

"Nifflers are often kept by goblins to burrow deep into the earth for treasure."

Fantastic Beasts and Where to Find Them

SPARKLY OBJECTS

Nifflers are drawn to shiny items. They can't resist collecting sparkly objects, although it isn't clear why they feel this need. In the film *Fantastic Beasts: The Crimes of Grindelwald*, Newt's Nifflers sleep in baskets filled with their glittering treasures.

NIFFLER JEWELLERY
PROP FROM THE FILM *FANTASTIC BEASTS: THE CRIMES OF GRINDELWALD*, 2018
Warner Bros.

FOOD STOCKPILE

Many pika species spend warmer periods harvesting a stockpile of flowers, grasses and mosses. This ensures that they will have enough plants stored away when there is less food around or when snow-covered ground makes food difficult to access.

ROYLE'S PIKA
Ochotona roylei
The Natural History Museum

Blue objects are particularly popular with satin bowerbirds. As blue is a rare colour in nature, this suggests that males who find lots of blue objects are perceived to be skilled, good-quality mates.

The Royle's pika's preferred food grows best with high rainfall and low temperatures. Climate change may cause a shortage of these plants, making it harder for the pika to find food and survive.

NIFFLER

"The Niffler is a British beast. Fluffy, black and long-snouted, this burrowing creature has a predilection for anything glittery. Nifflers are often kept by goblins to burrow deep into the earth for treasure. Though the Niffler is gentle and even affectionate, it can be destructive to belongings and should never be kept in a house. Nifflers live in lairs up to twenty feet below the surface and produce six to eight young in a litter."

Fantastic Beasts and Where to Find Them

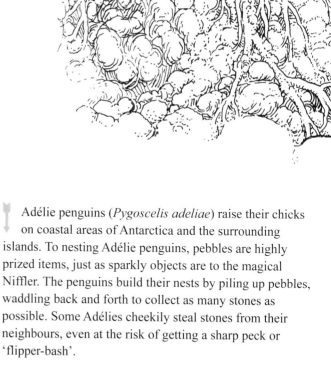

BASKET AND GLOVE

Need to recover an escaped Niffler? Newt's assistant, Bunty, dangles a shiny object from a glove to tempt a baby Niffler into her palm. Then she safely returns the creature to its treasure-filled basket.

BASKET AND GLOVE
PROP FROM THE FILM *FANTASTIC BEASTS: THE CRIMES OF GRINDELWALD*, 2018
Warner Bros.

Adélie penguins (*Pygoscelis adeliae*) raise their chicks on coastal areas of Antarctica and the surrounding islands. To nesting Adélie penguins, pebbles are highly prized items, just as sparkly objects are to the magical Niffler. The penguins build their nests by piling up pebbles, waddling back and forth to collect as many stones as possible. Some Adélies cheekily steal stones from their neighbours, even at the risk of getting a sharp peck or 'flipper-bash'.

Just like Nifflers, magpies (*Pica pica*) have a reputation for stealing shiny objects – in European folk tales, these birds are often seen as thieves. But a recent study may have proven magpies innocent. When presented with piles of shiny and non-shiny objects, magpies showed little interest and instead appeared afraid of new and unfamiliar things.

NATURAL DANCERS

Animal courtship is a world of colour, sound and motion. Bright feathers and patterns are often combined with lively dance moves. Complex, energetic routines help to show off the intelligence and fitness of a potential mate. Newt Scamander puts this knowledge to good use when he dances to attract an escaped female Erumpent in New York City.

Bobbing around the forests of its native central Papua New Guinea home, the male Lawes's parotia performs some flashy dance moves to attract a mate. This bird of paradise's forest home is increasingly threatened by logging and replacement by crops such as oil palm.

FEATHER 'TUTU' ⇒⇒

Fanning out its feathers, the male Lawes's parotia performs an intricate dance to impress potential mates. Female parotias watch from a branch above. When observing a similar species from the female bird's viewpoint, scientists discovered that the silvery feathers on the back of the male's head give a bright, mirror-like reflection, which emphasises its head movements during the mating dance.

FEMALE AND MALE LAWES'S PAROTIA (BIRD OF PARADISE)
Parotia lawesii
The Natural History Museum

ERUMPENT

> *The Erumpent is a large grey African beast of great power. Weighing up to a tonne, the Erumpent may be mistaken for a rhinoceros at a distance. It has a thick hide that repels most charms and curses, a large, sharp horn upon its nose and a long, rope-like tail. Erumpents give birth to only one calf at a time.*
>
> *The Erumpent will not attack unless sorely provoked, but should it charge, the results are usually catastrophic. The Erumpent's horn can pierce everything from skin to metal, and contains a deadly fluid which will cause whatever is injected with it to explode.*
>
> *Erumpent numbers are not great, as males frequently explode each other during the mating season. They are treated with great caution by African wizards. Erumpent horns, tails and the Exploding Fluid are all used in potions, though classified as Class B Tradeable Materials (Dangerous and Subject to Strict Control).*

Fantastic Beasts and Where to Find Them

ERUMPENT MUSK

Handle with care – Erumpent musk is potent! Newt uses just a few drops of musk (a type of scent) to catch the attention of a female Erumpent who has escaped into New York's Central Park Zoo. Newt then performs a mating dance to woo the Erumpent back into his magical case.

ERUMPENT MUSK

PROP FROM THE FILM
FANTASTIC BEASTS AND WHERE TO FIND THEM,
2016

Warner Bros.

Like the male Erumpent, the male peacock spider (*Maratus pavonis*), found in western and southern Australia, performs an elaborate mating dance. This little spider tries to wow females by raising and shaking its brightly coloured bottom (known as an abdomen) and waving its long, hairy legs in the air in a spectacular display of shimmering colour and choreographed movement. The delicate dance is a matter of life and death – if the female is not impressed, it might eat the male!

SHAPE-SHIFTERS

No animal can change size quite like the magical Occamy of the wizarding world, but nature still has its fair share of shape-shifters. Changing size or shape can be a handy survival tactic. Some animals shrink to save energy in harsh times or to squeeze into tight spaces. Others puff themselves up to look more threatening or less appealing to eat.

OCCAMY CATCHER

Occamies can change size dramatically to fit any available space. Newt uses a teapot to recover an escaped Occamy in New York City. By dropping a cockroach inside it as bait, the enormous Occamy is tempted to shrink to fit inside the teapot to get the tasty treat.

OCCAMY TEAPOT AND LID
PROP FROM THE FILM *FANTASTIC BEASTS AND WHERE TO FIND THEM*, 2016
Warner Bros.

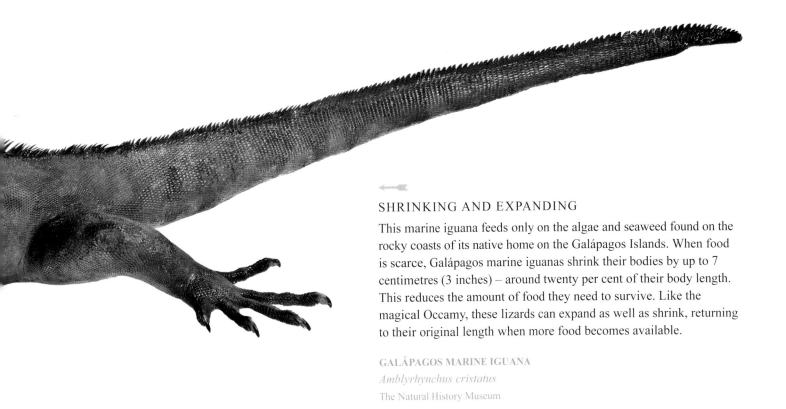

SHRINKING AND EXPANDING

This marine iguana feeds only on the algae and seaweed found on the rocky coasts of its native home on the Galápagos Islands. When food is scarce, Galápagos marine iguanas shrink their bodies by up to 7 centimetres (3 inches) – around twenty per cent of their body length. This reduces the amount of food they need to survive. Like the magical Occamy, these lizards can expand as well as shrink, returning to their original length when more food becomes available.

GALÁPAGOS MARINE IGUANA

Amblyrhynchus cristatus

The Natural History Museum

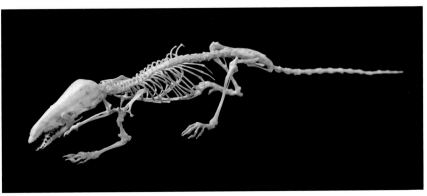

SHRINKING SKULL

A shrew's skull shrinks by around fifteen per cent between summer and winter. Scientists believe this is caused by bone tissue being reabsorbed from the joints between skull bones. Shrews can also shrink their spine, brain, heart and lungs. By making themselves smaller, it is thought that shrews will need less food and are more likely to survive the colder months.

COMMON SHREW AND SKELETON

Sorex araneus

The Natural History Museum

> *"A plumed, two-legged winged creature with a serpentine body, the Occamy may reach a length of fifteen feet."*

Fantastic Beasts and Where to Find Them

PAINTING OF AN OCCAMY (ETCHING WITH WATERCOLOUR)
OLIVIA LOMENECH GILL
Bloomsbury

CHAPTER SIX

MISUNDERSTOOD ANIMALS

"Imperfect understanding is often more dangerous than ignorance ..."

Newt Scamander

MISUNDERSTOOD ANIMALS

By Gillian Burke
Biologist and broadcaster

*Gillian Burke co-presents the BBC's wildlife series **Springwatch**, **Autumnwatch** and **Winterwatch**. She avidly champions the outcasts of the animal kingdom with past film credits including **Ultimate Guide to Spiders & Ants** for Discovery Channel and **King Cobra!** and **Anaconda!** for Animal Planet.*

Once there was a perfect little-girl-sized space hidden amongst a riot of ruby-red flowers, tucked away at the bottom of a hibiscus tree. As a child, I would spend hours there watching jewel-like sunbirds flit in and out of view. The little creatures would hover magically, levitating just at my eyeline, taking tiny sips of nectar until they had each had their fill.

Once the birds, with all their bright colours and flashy aerobatics, had moved on, I was left alone with the creeping, writhing and slithering creatures at my feet – quite literally. My childhood home was in Kenya and I hated wearing shoes! Despite grave warnings from all the grown-ups about the danger of 'jiggers' – parasitic insects that have the unpleasant habit of burrowing into human feet – I would tear around barefoot without a care in the world.

That's because, I would think to myself, *I don't trouble them and they don't trouble me!* To my adult self it may now seem reckless, but that's how I made sense of what must have simply been sheer good luck on the flesh-eating-insect front.

I imagine Newt Scamander would share this sentiment of embracing *all* of the fantastic beasts that roam the wizarding world. How else, other than by observing species at ease within their natural habitats, could he have earned their trust and learned so much about their behaviour? Occasionally he may have had to resort to defending himself with his travelling kettle if a specimen got a little too feisty, but even then, as a successful Magizoologist, he took care to show the same respect to a terrifying Acromantula or a lowly Flobberworm as would be fitting when bowing to a mighty Hippogriff or stroking a cuddly Puffskein.

The thing is, just as Newt Scamander could rely on a Bowtruckle or a Billywig, I could always count on the littlest creatures to show up and keep me company.

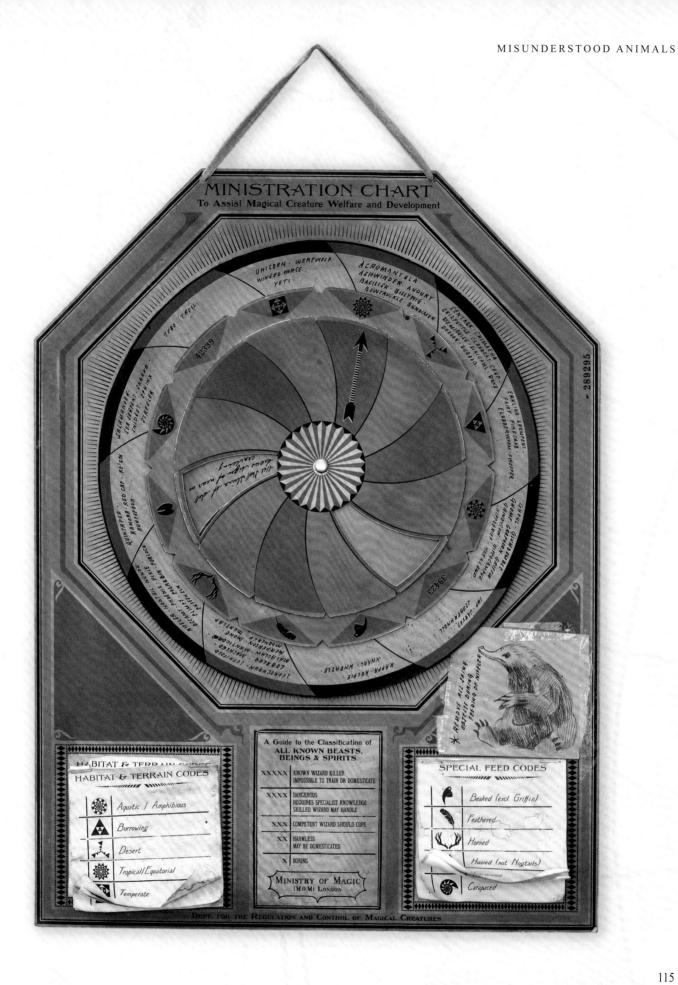

MINISTRATION CHART
To Assist Magical Creature Welfare and Development

A Guide to the Classification of
**ALL KNOWN BEASTS,
BEINGS & SPIRITS.**

XXXXX	KNOWN WIZARD KILLER IMPOSSIBLE TO TRAIN OR DOMESTICATE
XXXX	DANGEROUS REQUIRES SPECIALIST KNOWLEDGE SKILLED WIZARD MAY HANDLE
XXX	COMPETENT WIZARD SHOULD COPE
XX	HARMLESS MAY BE DOMESTICATED
X	BORING

MINISTRY OF MAGIC
(M.O.M) LONDON

HABITAT & TERRAIN CODES

	Aquatic / Amphibious
	Burrowing
	Desert
	Tropical/ Equatorial
	Temperate

SPECIAL FEED CODES

	Beaked (excl. Griffin)
	Feathered
	Horned
	Hooved (not Nogtails)
	Carapaced

REMOVE ALL JEWELLERY AND OBJECTS DURING FEEDING OF NIFFLER

DEPT. FOR THE REGULATION AND CONTROL OF MAGICAL CREATURES

Or maybe it was the other way round? I often used to crouch down to observe termite trails, my head down as near to the ground as I dared. As I gazed at the workers using their dainty mouthparts to delicately knead and mould their mud tunnels while the giant soldier termites stood guard over the colony, I knew *they knew* I was there. They could feel my breath when I moved in close – the soldier termites waving their massive heads and supersized jaws in proud defiance. The insects made it abundantly clear when I was getting too near, but as long as I kept a respectful distance they would tolerate my presence and carry on with their daily tasks of building, protecting and feeding the colony.

Watching termites expertly get on with the humdrum routine of their daily chores was my first clue that humans might not sit at the pinnacle of creation after all. Even more than that, the amazing innovation in the shape, size and specialisation of all the different worker castes within just one termite colony made me sit up and stare in utter astonishment at the incredible diversity surrounding me.

All of life is created equal, but it is not necessarily treated equally by us humans. Why are lions 'king of beasts' simply because of their magnificent manes while hyenas, with their untidy coats and hobbling gait, are often cast as the villains? Observing the great and the small, the cute and the grotesque, the predators and their prey, without judging one to be better than the other, is the most valuable lesson for any budding naturalist or Magizoologist.

I was able put this principle into practice years later when I worked as a research assistant at the Natural History Museum. My days began with my own version of platform nine and three-quarters as I slipped through a portal, courtesy of a concealed entrance, that allowed me to discreetly vanish from the visitors' section up a winding staircase and into the inner workings of the Museum.

I'd arrive at my destination, the Entomology Department, where a strong smell of mothballs accompanied the dizzying sight of rows and rows of wooden drawers worn to the warm patina that can only be acquired with extensive age and use. These drawers contained insect specimens collected from every corner of the globe – a precious record of the enormous diversity within just a single class of the animal kingdom.

I had been given the task of working through one miniscule portion of this vast collection. With each specimen, I would be transported to faraway lands and microscopic worlds where my mind was free to roam and piece together, like a detective, the forces that helped shape the insect into the mind-boggling variety that lay before me. My little evolutionary mind game threw into focus a myriad of continuous and unbroken lines connecting each and every living thing back to the earliest life forms while, at the same time, stretching into a future of endless possibilities. The view was nothing short of breathtaking.

For the first time I sensed, far beyond what my logical brain could appraise, the true value and beauty of each and every living thing. Each species is a record of life's inexhaustible response to the age-old challenge of staying alive. Each is a record of what's gone before, and the potential of species that are yet to exist.

It would be wise for us to humbly and quickly find our place in this beautifully complex web of life. We are uniquely placed to share, care for and protect all beasts – large, small, cute, strange or otherwise. Remember, as Newt himself said, "There are no strange creatures, only blinkered people."

STIGMATISED SPECIES

From howling wolves to flying vampire bats, from creeping hairy spiders to stealthy sharks with jaws packed full of razor-sharp teeth, many animals provoke fear and misunderstanding.

In the magical world of Newt Scamander, superstitions and beliefs influence the way fantastic beasts are treated. It is the same in our world – animals seen as evil or unlucky, or that pose a risk to humans, have been persecuted and, in some cases, reduced to very low populations.

Grey wolves, often associated with the sly 'Big Bad Wolf' of traditional Western folk tales or the terrifying predatory werewolf of mythology, have been hunted to extinction in many of the places where they once lived. Yet real wolves are extremely unlikely to attack humans.

Bats, such as the vampire bat and the flying fox, are seen as evil spirits or souls of the dead in some cultures, or are linked to the mythical blood-sucking monster Dracula. In reality, they are not the terrifying flying monsters of the night as imagined – they are highly social creatures, sharing their food with other bats that have not managed to feed, and playing a vital role in pollinating and transporting fruit tree seeds.

Human activity is endangering the future of many of our animals, with hundreds of thousands of species at risk of disappearing forever. Newt Scamander rescues, protects and cares for fantastic beasts that are threatened, mistreated or misunderstood by other wizards, such as the magnificent Zouwu. Like Newt, a diverse range of scientists, conservationists and local communities are working to protect threatened species. They hope to minimise the conflicts between people and animals that are a potential danger to lives or livelihoods, and to transform the way we think about stigmatised creatures, securing a future where we can live alongside each other with respect and acceptance, rather than fear.

"It is my fondest hope that a new generation of witches and wizards will find in its pages fresh reason to love and protect the incredible beasts with whom we share magic."

Fantastic Beasts and Where to Find Them

NEWT'S ENCHANTED BASEMENT

When he's on the move, Newt uses his magical case to house and care for fantastic beasts. Back home in London, his enchanted basement serves as a hospital filled with tools to keep his creatures healthy and happy. Items range from eye drops for Mooncalves to feeding bottles for baby Nifflers.

MOONCALF EYEDROPPER AND NIFFLER FEEDING BOTTLE

PROPS FROM THE FILM *FANTASTIC BEASTS: THE CRIMES OF GRINDELWALD*, 2018

Warner Bros.

Today, thanks to conservation work and a better understanding of grey wolves (*Canis lupus*), the species as a whole isn't under threat, with several populations recovering in areas where they were once hunted. However, these incredible, intelligent creatures are not out of danger yet, as some populations are still classified as endangered and some subspecies are already extinct.

Names have a big impact on how we view animals. The vampire bat (*Desmodus rotundus*) is automatically linked to the mythical blood-sucking monster of its name. Although it can carry rabies, the vampire bat has rarely been known to bite humans. In fact, humans are more of a threat to this species, chopping down the forests where it lives and destroying its natural habitat.

CASPIAN TIGER

As forests shrink and cities expand, large predators like tigers are encountering people ever more frequently. As with the magical Zouwu, these confrontations can be dangerous for humans and big cats alike. The Caspian tiger is a victim of this conflict. Once found across Central Asia, this subspecies was driven to extinction in the 1970s as humans replaced its habitat with farms and cities. For the world's wild tigers to survive, we need to find new ways of living peacefully alongside big cats.

CASPIAN TIGER
Panthera tigris virgata
The Natural History Museum

Some tiger populations are increasing, but they now exist in only four per cent of the areas where they once lived. Total tiger numbers were reduced from around 100,000 individuals in 1910 to around 3,900 in 2016. Attacks on people and livestock mean communities are under pressure to prioritise their families over protecting vulnerable populations of tigers, like the Bengal tiger (*Panthera tigris tigris*). Conservationists are working with these communities to create win-win solutions for both humans and animals, where saving wildlife promotes safe and sustainable living.

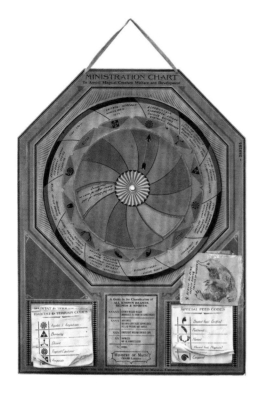

FEEDING MAGICAL CREATURES

This chart provides care advice for all of the magical creatures in Newt's book *Fantastic Beasts and Where to Find Them*. It includes guidelines for feeding animals with beaks, feathers, horns, hooves and carapaces (hard shells). The hand-drawn sketch pinned at the side includes a note to "remove all shiny objects during feeding of Niffler".

MINISTRATION CHART TO ASSIST MAGICAL CREATURE WELFARE AND DEVELOPMENT
PROP FROM THE FILM *FANTASTIC BEASTS AND WHERE TO FIND THEM*, 2016
Warner Bros.

TAMING THE ZOUWU

The Zouwu is a cat-like, magical creature from China. The size of an elephant, it is incredibly powerful and fast. When a Zouwu escapes onto the streets of Paris in *Fantastic Beasts: The Crimes of Grindelwald*, it is a danger to itself and those around it. Luckily, Newt is able to guide it to safety. He shakes a feathery toy at it and then drops the toy into his case. The Zouwu jumps into the case to chase the toy.

ZOUWU TOY
PROP FROM THE FILM *FANTASTIC BEASTS: THE CRIMES OF GRINDELWALD*, 2018
Warner Bros.

FIRE-BREATHER

In this original artwork for the Illustrated Edition of *Harry Potter and the Goblet of Fire*, artist Jim Kay paints the Hungarian Horntail dragon in its full, fire-breathing glory. The scene shows a defensive female Horntail guarding a golden egg. Harry was tasked with stealing this egg in his first challenge of the Triwizard Tournament.

Newt describes Hungarian Horntails as supposedly the most dangerous of the ten dragon breeds. Known to feed on humans, they can breathe fire up to 15 metres (50 feet). To keep people safe, some dragons in the wizarding world are kept hidden in special reserves. Occasionally they fly outside these areas in search of prey, putting them at risk of conflict with humans.

PAINTING OF THE HUNGARIAN
HORNTAIL DRAGON

JIM KAY

Bloomsbury

CHAPTER SEVEN

ENDANGERED SPECIES

"We should be protecting these creatures instead of killing them."

Newt Scamander

ENDANGERED SPECIES

By Patrick Barkham
Author and journalist

*Patrick Barkham is an award-winning author and natural history writer for
the **Guardian**. His books include **The Butterfly Isles**, **Badgerlands** and **Islander**.
His latest, **Wild Child**, is about the joy children can find in everyday nature.*

In the middle of the Indian Ocean lies a speck of volcanic soil clothed in tropical green. This small island, Mauritius, is the birthplace of extinction – the permanent vanishing of species from planet Earth. But it is also a place of great hope, where we have learned how to bring rare animals back from the brink.

Having visited over a hundred countries across the globe, I imagine that Newt Scamander may have been equally fascinated by this lonely, tropical isle. The first known visitors were Dutch seafarers arriving in 1598. Isolated from other countries and continents for millions of years, fantastic creatures had been able to evolve here, including a large, flightless pigeon – the dodo.

Yet within a century of people setting up home on Mauritius, the dodo was driven to extinction. Settlers' companion animals, the pigs and black rats they brought with them, destroyed the dodo's habitat and ate the eggs of the defenceless birds that previously lived in a pig-less, rat-less, people-less paradise.

A replica of the dodo – known as the Diricawl to those in the wizarding world – is a star exhibit in the Natural History Museum. It is a symbol of an era of extinction – a reproach and a reminder. Scientists propose that our era of geological time should be called the Anthropocene. It means that the planet and its inhabitants are shaped by one dominant species: *Homo sapiens*. One feature of this age is that Earth is losing its bewitching diversity of life more quickly than in the past many millions of years. We have commenced what some call the Sixth Great Extinction.

We know today that a million species are threatened with extinction. There is also a great loss of abundance. Epic swarms of monarch butterflies, great murmurations of starlings and huge herds of wildebeest are becoming rarer. Three billion birds have vanished from the skies of the USA and Canada since 1970. In Britain, more than a quarter of native birds are in danger of extinction or are experiencing significant

declines. The turtle dove is most at risk – its numbers have plummeted by ninety-eight per cent since 1970. There are barely a thousand breeding pairs left in the UK.

In recent years, the baiji, a unique and marvellous 20 million-year-old species of river dolphin, has vanished from the Yangtze River in China – and is now believed to be extinct. A small bat, the Christmas Island pipistrelle, has disappeared forever from its remote Australian island home. The po'o-uli, or black-faced honeycreeper, a pretty bird with a striking black mask across its eyes, has become extinct on the Hawaiian island of Maui.

Each species disappears because of a unique set of circumstances, but there are also common causes. Almost every extinction is linked to human action. A few animals are hunted because we make money from them. The horn of the white rhino, for example, has reputed power in traditional medicines. Most, however, are accidental extinctions. We don't deliberately drive these creatures into oblivion, but unfortunately we all unwittingly play a small part. Our consumption of planet Earth's resources is growing. As our population expands and we live more lavishly, so we take more wild space – for farming, mining, industry, roads and houses – and pollute soil and sea. We squeeze other animals onto ever smaller fragments of land or water. We also move species around the world. These 'invasive' species – particularly cats, but also dogs, foxes, mongooses, rats and mice – often wipe out creatures that have evolved without defences against these new predators.

An extinction is like a death – it is sad and depressing. But alongside this pattern of loss and destruction is a more hopeful, heartening happening. We have become the first ever brutish beast to consciously work to save other animals from extinction. Each year, we become better at it. We are bringing hundreds of endangered species back from the edge. In the wizarding world, the Golden Snidget was once almost hunted to extinction by wizards for its feathers and jewel-red eyes, which are highly prized. Luckily the danger was recognised in time and the species protected by stringent measures including the introduction of Snidget sanctuaries. The lesson for wizards and Muggles alike is simple – we can save every single rare animal, if we really try.

Over the last century, there have been thousands of heroes in the emerging field of conservation science. Advocates who, just like Newt Scamander, have devoted their lives to saving species.

Great efforts have also been made on the island of Mauritius. In the latter decades of the twentieth century, there were fewer than twelve known wild specimens of five different bird species on the tropical island. On the brink of extinction, the Mauritius kestrel, the pink pigeon, the echo parakeet, the Rodrigues fody and the Rodrigues warbler were widely expected to follow the dodo.

Saving species is always a team effort, but last-ditch captive breeding efforts led by Carl Jones, a Welsh conservation scientist, helped save all these five endangered animals. By understanding what the birds needed to breed more successfully, restoring forest habitats and controlling predators, the rarest birds of Mauritius are today living wild in their hundreds and sometimes thousands.

It is easy to feel powerless but individuals *can* make a difference. The large blue butterfly became extinct in Britain in 1979. Fortunately, this species clung on in some European countries and Professor Jeremy Thomas collected caterpillars from Sweden and set about restoring the insect to Britain. By learning exactly what made the large blue tick – a fascinating symbiotic relationship with a species of ant – he was able to recreate suitable meadowland habitat. Today, each June, more large blues fly in south-west England than anywhere else in the world.

Some people may wonder, what is the point of saving one apparently insignificant butterfly species? Isn't it irrelevant when we are losing so much? The act of saving one species, however, always requires us to understand and restore its wider ecosystem. By rescuing one species, we benefit hundreds of others.

Some of us will argue that saving species ultimately enables us to survive – other animals and plants are the source of food or life-saving medicines, or they perform crucial 'ecosystem services' such as pollination to sustain life on Earth. For others, it is a moral imperative. Every species with whom we share our miraculous planet has a right to be here. Saving them is simply the right thing to do. As Newt also remarks in his instructive foreword to *Fantastic Beasts and Where to Find Them*, our endeavours to protect wildlife are not just undertaken for our own benefit – they are a legacy for future generations. Our descendants also deserve to delight in nature's riches, just as we have done.

We Muggles can all agree that saving species brings us alive to the joy and wonder of *our* world. We don't have to simply be a problem child for the planet – we can become a saviour with a solution.

THE HUMAN IMPACT

Many animal species have been reduced to very low populations and are on the brink of extinction because of human activities such as poaching and the illegal trading of animal body parts. Tusks, horns, skins, feathers and bones are all considered valuable commodities. Animals are exploited for their perceived commercial value – they are killed for their meat or to make fashion items, trinkets or medicines. Helmeted hornbills, elephants, rhinoceroses and pangolins, to name a few, have been the victims of the cruel trade in ivory, meat, and horns and scales for unproven 'medicinal' cures. Vaquita porpoises have suffered devastating losses in their numbers at the hands of illegal fishing. In fact, this now rare creature may well be extinct by the time you read this.

Like Newt, scientists and conservationists are working hard, often against the odds, to help protect vulnerable, rare and endangered species from overexploitation and to prevent their extinction. Their job isn't easy. Restoring a healthy population after a species has been reduced to a small number of individuals is a challenge. Intensive breeding programmes are helping to increase the numbers of some animals, for example, the New Zealand kākāpō parrot. In the wizarding world, Newt manages to rescue the last breeding pair of Graphorns in existence.

Increased public awareness and education have played an important role in reducing the demand for animal parts. However, more still needs to be done. Protecting an endangered species also requires the support and collaboration of governments, law enforcement agencies and local communities. Targeted campaigns using posters and other media platforms help to raise awareness of the real threats endangered animals face and to generate support for conservation efforts. And with the advances in technology, scientists are able to track and monitor vulnerable species, providing invaluable research for the continued protection of the amazing creatures with whom we share our planet.

Elephants are hunted and either killed or maimed for their ivory tusks. Many welfare organisations and charities work tirelessly to protect these incredible animals, and to try to end the unnecessary and cruel ivory trade.

THREATENED BY TRADE

Having an amazing horn or beak, beautiful feathers or scales, or laying appealing eggs can be a real hazard in the animal world. Sadly, many creatures with these incredible assets are exploited by humans, just for their commercial trade value.

> *"The Department for the Regulation and Control of Magical Creatures keeps a strict watch on the trade in fantastic beasts."*
>
> *Fantastic Beasts and Where to Find Them*

SUNDA PANGOLIN

Pangolins are covered in hard scales made of keratin, which help protect them from predators. These scales are highly sought after as ingredients in traditional medicines. There is no scientific evidence to support belief in their medicinal powers, and it is estimated that over a million pangolins have been killed in recent decades for their scales as well as their meat. From organising patrols to stop poachers to rescuing trafficked animals, many people are working together to keep these scaly mammals alive in the wild.

All species of pangolin are protected by law, and several species are critically endangered. These incredible animals are not well-understood – scientists and conservationists are working to learn more about their breeding and living habits, and to identify poaching hotspots as well as to reduce consumer demand for their scales and meat.

SUNDA PANGOLIN
Manis javanica
The Natural History Museum

ERUMPENT HORN

In the wizarding world, the large, sharp horns of Erumpents are used as ingredients in potions. In *Fantastic Beasts and Where to Find Them*, Newt writes that Erumpent populations are low, but does not explain how trade in their horns might impact this magical species.

ERUMPENT HORN SEEN IN THE LOVEGOOD HOME
PROP FROM THE FILM *HARRY POTTER AND THE DEATHLY HALLOWS – PART 1*, 2010
Warner Bros.

Pangolins eat ants and termites using their incredibly long, sticky tongues. They can roll up into a tight ball to protect themselves when threatened by predators. There are eight species of pangolin, four in Asia and four in Africa. They range from vulnerable to critically endangered.

Over the last few years, hundreds of tonnes of pangolin scales, shipped and traded illegally, have been intercepted. The shy, scaly creature is the world's most trafficked mammal.

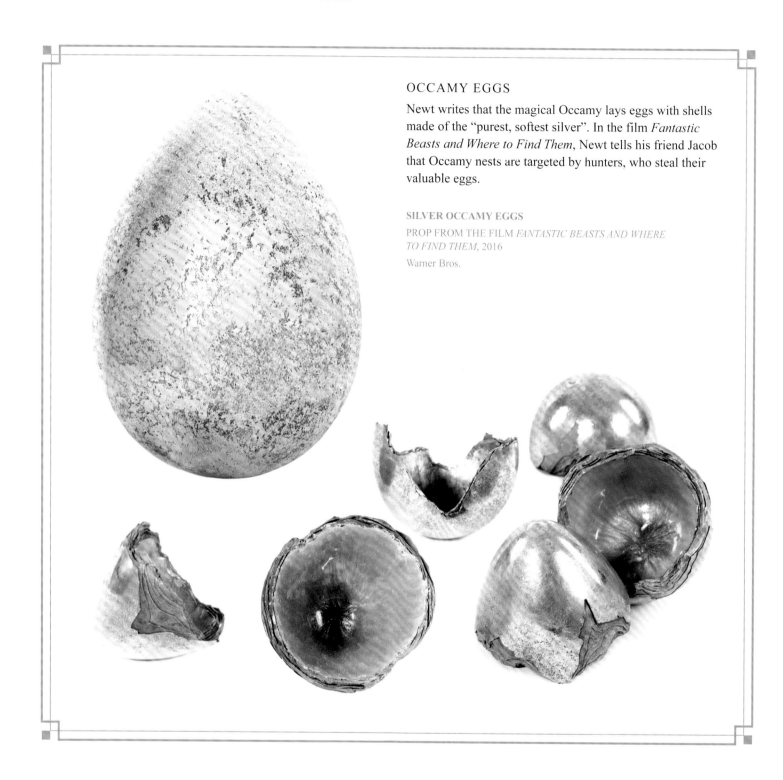

OCCAMY EGGS

Newt writes that the magical Occamy lays eggs with shells made of the "purest, softest silver". In the film *Fantastic Beasts and Where to Find Them*, Newt tells his friend Jacob that Occamy nests are targeted by hunters, who steal their valuable eggs.

SILVER OCCAMY EGGS
PROP FROM THE FILM *FANTASTIC BEASTS AND WHERE TO FIND THEM*, 2016
Warner Bros.

> " *The Occamy is aggressive to all who approach it, particularly in defence of its eggs, whose shells are made of the purest, softest silver.* "

Fantastic Beasts and Where to Find Them

HUNTED ⤐

Once widespread in the forests of Southeast Asia, the helmeted hornbill is being hunted to extinction for the hard, bony casque above its beak, which can be carved like ivory. Like the Occamy's silver eggs, carved hornbill casques are highly valued in some countries. In recent years, this has led to a surge in hunting. Almost 3,000 casques have been seized in the last decade, but that is only a tiny part of the global illegal trade. Conservationists are now working to enforce bans on hunting and trading, and to reduce demand for hornbill products. Local conservation programmes work with communities to try to convert poachers into rangers to protect the species.

CASQUE OF A HELMETED HORNBILL,
CARVED IN THE 1800s
Rhinoplax vigil
The Natural History Museum

Helmeted hornbills play an important role in tropical forests by spreading seeds from the figs they eat. This helps new fruit trees grow, and these provide food for many other species.

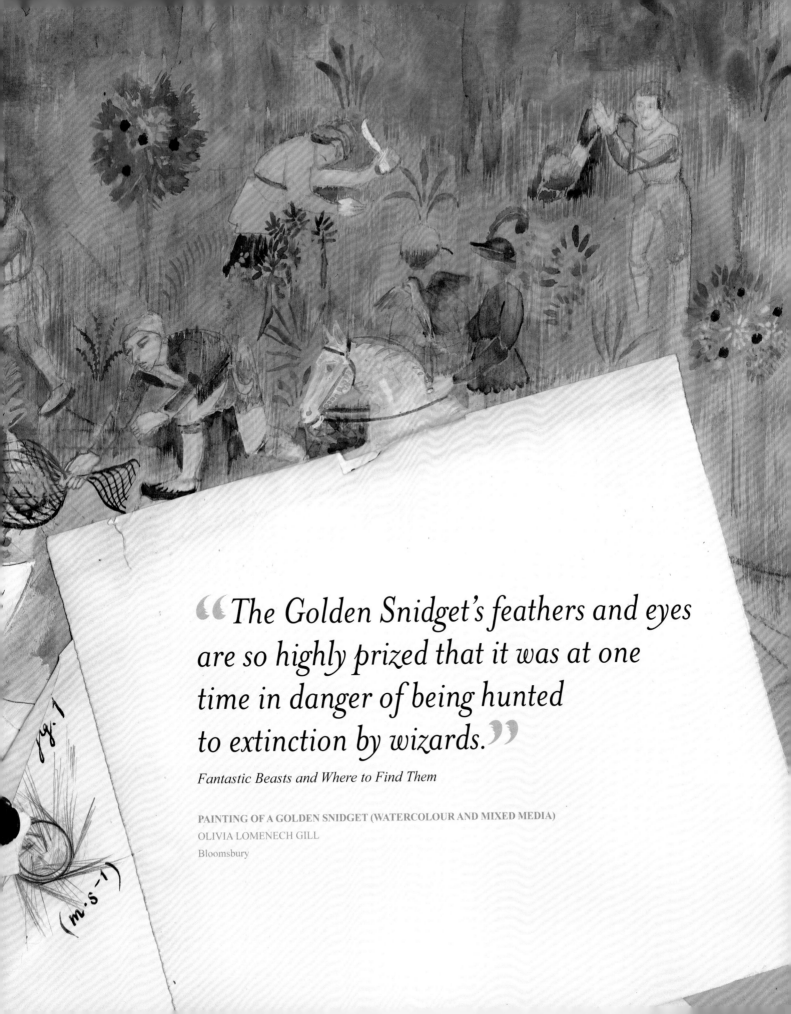

“ *The Golden Snidget's feathers and eyes
are so highly prized that it was at one
time in danger of being hunted
to extinction by wizards.* ”

Fantastic Beasts and Where to Find Them

PAINTING OF A GOLDEN SNIDGET (WATERCOLOUR AND MIXED MEDIA)
OLIVIA LOMENECH GILL
Bloomsbury

SAVING A SPECIES

In *Fantastic Beasts and Where to Find Them*, Newt explains that he has saved the wizarding world's last pair of Graphorns from the brink of extinction. Under his care, these horned, hump-backed beasts produce a new generation of baby Graphorns, giving hope for the future of this magical species. Newt also tries to educate his fellow wizards – Graphorns are killed for both their horns and their thick, spell-proof skins.

In our world, many animal species like the vaquita porpoise and the kākāpō parrot have come close to being wiped out altogether because of human activities such as fishing and hunting. Scientists and conservationists are working urgently to save them from extinction.

The vaquita (*Phocoena sinus*) is the world's smallest porpoise and one of the most endangered species on our planet. Vaquitas live off the coast of Mexico, where they are often caught accidentally in illegal fishing nets. Like the magical Graphorn, vaquita populations have fallen to very low numbers. Conservationists have tried everything from captive breeding at sea to redesigning fishing gear in order to keep this species from disappearing forever. As of 2019, it was thought that fewer than twenty vaquitas were left in the world. Researchers fear that if we do not act urgently to save this precious porpoise, this species could become extinct in the next few years, or even months.

TECHNOLOGIES TO SAVE A SPECIES

Conservationists working with New Zealand's Kākāpō Recovery Programme use specially developed technologies to monitor the location and health of every kākāpō in the reserves. Each kākāpō wears a radio transmitter like a miniature rucksack. These devices send scientists information about the birds' activities, such as mating and nesting. The researchers monitor each kākāpō's diet using electronically controlled feeding stations, and they remove kākāpō eggs from nests so they can be cared for and incubated safely. They leave smart eggs that make lifelike sounds in their place so that kākāpō mothers can prepare for the arrival of their chicks.

The kākāpō (*Strigops habroptila*) is a flightless, nocturnal parrot that was once found all over New Zealand. Today only a small population remains. The kākāpō came close to extinction in the late twentieth century. This followed many years of hunting by people and the cats, rats and stoats introduced to the islands by human settlers. Conservationists moved all remaining birds to predator-free reserves in the 1980s, launching an intensive breeding programme to help save the species. Between 1995 and 2020, conservationists have helped increase kākāpō numbers from fifty-one to over 200 birds.

**"They're the last breeding pair in existence.
If I hadn't managed to rescue them, that could
have been the end of Graphorns — for ever."**

Fantastic Beasts and Where to Find Them
(2016 film)

PAINTING OF A GRAPHORN (WATERCOLOUR AND MIXED MEDIA)
OLIVIA LOMENECH GILL
Bloomsbury

ADVOCATES FOR OUR PLANET

An advocate for the planet is someone who speaks up on behalf of nature and ultimately will take action to protect it. Over the last few years there has been an increase in youth activists around the world. Millions of young people have joined strikes, marches and rallies to demand that nations act now to fight global warming and other environmental and animal issues that affect all living creatures. Take a look at some of the inspirational advocates for our planet who are working to make the world a better place.

Greta Thunberg

Swedish teenage climate change activist. Greta sparked a global awakening with her school strike protests ('Fridays for Future'), and her international environmental campaigns and rallies to demand a change before it is too late. In one of her rally speeches, she told the world that "our house is on fire", because we only have about twelve years before the effects of climate change become irreversible.

Zero Hour

A US climate change youth movement started in 2017 by Jamie Margolin, Nadia Nazar, Madelaine Tew and Zanagee Artis. The teenage founders wanted to force global leaders and adults around the world to listen to their real worries about the impact climate change will have on our planet and all of nature, and the potential destruction of their future home.

Bella Lack

British teenage environmental activist and youth ambassador for the Born Free Foundation, which works to ensure all wild animals (and those in captivity) are treated with compassion and respect and are able to live their lives according to their needs. Bella's petition against the use of wild animals in UK circuses spurred a government ban.

Dara McAnulty

British teenage naturalist, conservationist and passionate advocate for wildlife. Dara dedicates all of his spare time to campaigning for wildlife, in particular persecuted birds of prey. He also visits schools and speaks at conferences working to encourage young people to connect with nature and to promote the wonders of our natural world. He has written about the challenges facing the planet in his book *Diary of a Young Naturalist*.

Malaika Vaz

Wildlife presenter and filmmaker, activist, conservationist and National Geographic Explorer from Goa, India. Still only in her twenties, Malaika has already made her mark as an advocate for the planet, filming documentaries on the human–tiger conflict in Central India and illegal trading in manta and mobula rays. She has been on research expeditions to Antarctica and the Arctic, and is also known for hosting *On the Brink*, an eight-part series about extinction, as well as a three-part series called *Living with Predators*.

Georgia Locock

British young conservationist and blogger. When not studying, Georgia spends her time campaigning about issues that threaten our natural environment. She visits schools to promote the importance of conservation, and makes films to highlight issues such as illegal badger culling and the mass slaughtering of migratory birds.

"*Newt Scamander was awarded the Order of Merlin, Second Class, in 1979 in recognition of his services to the study of magical beasts, Magizoology.*"

Fantastic Beasts and Where to Find Them

CHAPTER EIGHT

SAVING OUR NATURAL WORLD

*"The danger was recognised in time
and the species protected ..."*

Newt Scamander

SAVING OUR NATURAL WORLD

By Mya-Rose Craig
Birder, naturalist and conservationist

Mya-Rose Craig is a passionate ornithologist, campaigner for equal rights and diversity, and the creator of the non-profit organisation Black2Nature. Mya-Rose is the youngest person to be awarded an honorary doctorate in science from the University of Bristol. To her many social media followers, she is also known as 'Birdgirl'.

In my search to see and document bird species I have been on many journeys. Just like Newt Scamander, I have been fortunate enough to visit dark jungles and bright deserts, mountain peaks and marshy bogs. I have not, as yet, had to use my travelling kettle to fight off a monster, although it may have come in useful during the time I was in South Africa searching for a Pel's fishing owl.

I was trekking with my family through the forest near a river, looking for the owl. I was only four, my legs were short and my mum and I had fallen behind the rest of the group. When the guide suddenly turned and motioned for quiet, we assumed that my dad and sister were already watching the owl without us. We both started running to catch up. At that ill-fated moment, we also heard a massive crashing sound in the trees – a large hippopotamus was charging towards us through the undergrowth.

Hippos are the most dangerous animals in Africa, with far more yearly deaths under their belt than any lion or crocodile. You should never get between a hippo and where it wants to be, but that was exactly where my mum and I were now standing. We tried to run away, but in our panic tripped over each other, our legs tangled. We both fell, directly into the path of the rampaging beast. My dad, overcome by the prospect of our imminent demise, rushed over in a panic and threw himself on top of us. I found myself squashed at the bottom of a human pile, my heart pounding. (My sister Ayesha, apparently the only sensible one in the family, had stuck with the guide.) As the hippo rapidly approached, we braced for the end.

Thankfully it didn't come. At the very last possible moment our guide ran towards the animal yelling so furiously that the hippo was startled and swerved around the mass of tangled limbs, missing us by less than a metre. It was a terrifying brush with death, all in the quest for an owl.

But then, as you can tell, I *really* love birds. Their beautiful plumage and seemingly magical ability to take to the skies have always been fascinating to me. They are, in my view, the most fantastic of beasts. I simply cannot remember a time when birds weren't part of my life. Sometimes photographs implant a scene in your brain, and many of my early birding memories are like this. I have an album with a few old photographs. The first is a slightly crumpled shot of me as a tiny nine-day-old baby peering into a telescope, held up by my older sister. It was a sign of how the rest of my life was going to pan out: squinting through telescopic eyepieces and binoculars, perennially on the lookout.

I have managed to track down over half of the birds in the world during my extensive travels, from the giant harpy eagle of South and Central America – a bird that stands nearly a metre tall with claws the size of dinner plates – to the tiniest of hummingbirds, my favourite being the sword-billed hummingbird which has a bill longer than its body and the ability to fly backwards like the magical and rare Golden Snidget. Some of the birds I've spotted transport me back to prehistoric times. The hoatzin from the Amazon resembles an *Archaeopteryx*, the missing link between dinosaurs and birds. Their young have hooked claws on their wings to help them climb through the trees. I have also seen the bones of the giant elephant bird of Madagascar. Standing three metres tall and weighing in at over 700 kilograms, they were the largest birds to ever have roamed the Earth.

Some of today's birds can be menacing and dangerous. The southern cassowary from Australia can kill a person with a single kick. Some, like golden parrots and birds of paradise, can be unutterably gorgeous, with their jewel-toned feathers and exotic dance displays. Many can be intelligent and nurturing – the maleo buries its eggs in earth warmed by hot springs, while penguins balance their chicks on their feet to protect them from the cold.

Of all the creatures of our world, however, the most fantastic I've ever seen has a beak and lays eggs, but isn't a bird at all. The duck-billed platypus dwells in the quiet streams of eastern Australia. It is such a strange-looking creature that the first time scientists saw one they thought it was a prank. The platypus is shy and gentle, but it is equipped with venomous spurs for defence. It seals itself inside a burrow to lay eggs, and has 'sixth sense' electroreceptors in its bill, which allows the platypus to locate prey in dark waters using the electric signals generated by its heartbeat. With the recent bushfire disaster in Australia, researchers say these endangered animals could be lost during the coming decades. This, like any and every extinction, would be a catastrophe. It is something that we must fight against with all our collective might.

Saving our natural world is the most important challenge for my generation and something that Newt himself was already fighting for long ago. We need to act now to stop climate breakdown and species extinction before it becomes too late. As a young person faced with such devastatingly vital and urgent issues, it's easy to feel angry, anxious, depressed, defeated even. What can we do to help? Where do we start?

I believe that it is possible to turn things around, one step at a time. The first thing we must do to succeed is come together. To do that, nature enthusiasts and naturalists like me have to work to engage *all* people from every background, all over the world.

During my early years as a birder I quickly realised how fortunate I was to have had the opportunity to experience the wonders of the natural world up close. I am part Bangladeshi, and I was also aware that there weren't many people who looked like me spending time out in nature. In the summer of 2015, when I was thirteen, I decided to do something about this. I came up with a plan to arrange a nature camp especially for ethnic minority teenagers. It was a simple concept, but very difficult to execute, yet the response was amazing. The participants' reactions proved that by making nature relevant, everyone can enjoy it. Empowering these teenagers to fight for the environment also gave them the tools to campaign in other positive ways – for equality and against racism. Since then I've put on more camps and in 2016 founded Black2Nature, an organisation dedicated to enabling ethnic minority children and teenagers to enjoy the great outdoors. I sincerely believe that prioritising diversity is a great step towards bringing people together in the fight to create a sustainable world.

So what can *you* do to help save our dazzling planet? Start by stepping outside. You may not be in the Andes mountains or in an African savannah, but chances are you have some woods, a field or a park nearby. You may not have a garden or yard, but even the tiniest window box can attract fascinating minibeasts and visiting birds. Newt Scamander finds magic anywhere and everywhere. So can you.

Come on, get out there. Breathe, walk, watch, listen. The wonders of nature await.

Mya-Rose Craig

HOPE FOR THE FUTURE

The alarming words, "The future of the natural world, on which we all depend, is in your hands", spoken recently at a climate change conference by Sir David Attenborough, the renowned naturalist, writer and broadcaster, have never been more relevant. Today, we face a planetary emergency. Humanity's future depends on the natural world, but unsustainable human activity is causing multiple global environmental crises. Climate change; biodiversity loss and extinctions; habitat destruction; plastic, water and air pollution; erosion; soil loss; deforestation; desertification; ocean acidification and the loss of coral reefs, to name a few of the crises, are the direct result of our actions. By threatening Earth's natural systems, we threaten our own future. We must act now and we must act together, for a future where both people and the planet thrive.

Conservationists and naturalists like Sir David, scientists, activists and many other organisations and inspirational individuals around the globe are already working hard to make a sustainable planet a reality. Like them, Newt Scamander's tireless work to protect all fantastic creatures in the wizarding world also helps promote an understanding and appreciation of the wonders of the natural world. Newt might not have the technology or media platforms we have today, but of course he does have magic on his side.

Whether wizard or Muggle, we all need to do more to protect our worlds. Our planet's ecology has never been in such a critical state as it is today, yet never have we been better equipped with the tools to understand what is happening and what needs to be done. Changes in our behaviour and direct action based on the knowledge and understanding that emerges from scientific discovery are the way forward. Understanding life on our planet is an immense scientific challenge, but it is also the way in which we can successfully predict, plan and effect change. Empowering people to make informed and sustainable choices will make a positive difference to the global future, and a world where we can enjoy all the natural beauty around us. Newt would be proud of us!

Blue whales (*Balaenoptera musculus*) were hunted to the brink of extinction in the twentieth ⟫→ century, but were also one of the first species that humans decided to save on a global scale. In 1966 there were only around 400 thought to be left in the world, but since then the population has steadily grown to its current level of around 20,000. The Natural History Museum has a stunning 25.2-metre-long (82.7 feet) female blue whale skeleton suspended from the ceiling in one of their main exhibition halls. They have named her Hope as a symbol of humanity's power to shape a sustainable future.

SUCCESS STORIES

The invaluable work of conservationists around the world is helping to save many endangered species, and provides hope for other threatened wildlife. Some animals have been brought back from the brink of extinction. Creatures like the blue whale, the giant panda and the mountain gorilla are still here, with their numbers slowly increasing, thanks to conservation efforts. Habitat restoration, protected wildlife reserves and captive breeding programmes, hunting bans and the enforcement of laws against illegal trading of animals are all helping to protect vulnerable animals.

In the 1980s excessive poaching and deforestation decimated China's population of giant pandas (*Ailuropoda melanoleuca*), reducing their numbers to as few as 1,114. However it wasn't until only a few hundred bears remained that a global movement to save them began. A panda census is taken every ten to fifteen years to keep track of their numbers. The most recent survey was carried out in 2014 and it estimated that there were 1,864 pandas living in the wild, and about another 300 in zoos and breeding centres around the world. Nearly two thirds of all wild pandas now live in protected wildlife reserves and a handful of captive-bred pandas has been released into the wild. The panda's long-term safety is not yet secure, but with the hard work of the Chinese government, local communities, wildlife organisations like the World Wildlife Fund (WWF) and conservation workers, the giant panda's future is looking brighter.

Combined conservation efforts between various wildlife organisations and local African governments are making a huge difference to endangered gorilla (*Gorilla beringei beringei*) populations. Sanctuaries and protected areas have been set up in many places, with monitoring programmes being carried out by park rangers, and better environmental practices being encouraged to prevent habitat destruction by deforestation for mining and agriculture. The number of mountain gorillas has continued to increase in recent years, leading to its downlisting from critically endangered to endangered in November 2018. The results of the most recent survey conducted in 2018 in a national park in Uganda, combined with the results from the 2015/2016 Virunga Massif survey, which monitors mountain gorillas in Eastern Africa, list the global total of wild mountain gorillas as 1,063.

"In the meantime I will merely add that it affords me great pleasure to think that generations of young witches and wizards have grown to a fuller knowledge and understanding of the fantastic beasts I love through the pages of this book."

Fantastic Beasts and Where to Find Them

153

LOUIS BUCKLEY

Louis is Lead Curator of *Fantastic Beasts: The Wonder of Nature*. He has a background in zoology, science journalism and interaction design and has worked on exhibitions exploring subjects as diverse as the history of spying, antibiotic resistance, and biohacking. Like Newt, Louis is a Hufflepuff who has been fascinated by animals from a young age, and he has a particular affection for frogs and other pond-dwelling creatures. His Patronus is a mastiff dog and his wand is made of sycamore wood, with a phoenix-feather core.

LORRAINE CORNISH

Lorraine is Head of Conservation at the Natural History Museum and coordinated the input from the Museum scientists for *Fantastic Beasts: The Wonder of Nature*. She has a background in geology, conservation and exhibition development. Lorraine has worked on projects such as the conservation of Hope the blue whale skeleton, which hangs in the Museum's Hintze Hall. Lorraine is a Slytherin, but unlike Draco Malfoy is opposed to bullying in all its forms. She has long been fascinated by sea monsters and thinks that spiders are misunderstood. Her Patronus is a rat and her wand is made of walnut wood, with a unicorn-hair core.

ANNA DARRON

Anna co-curated *Fantastic Beasts: The Wonder of Nature*, researching content, developing exhibits and selecting objects and specimens for display. A proud Hufflepuff with a background in anthropology and cultural heritage studies, she has previously worked on exhibitions about cravings and appetite, humanoid robots, and the sun. Anna dreamed of working in a natural history museum from a young age, but never imagined just how magical it would be! When not behind the scenes, she can be found outdoors, hiking or travelling with her acacia wood, phoenix-feather core wand (quite bendy) close to hand. Her Patronus is a Russian wolfhound.

KATE WHITTINGTON

Kate co-curated *Fantastic Beasts: The Wonder of Nature*, developing content and creating exhibits to bring the real and magical worlds to life. She has a background in environmental science, science communication and wildlife illustration. Kate has worked on local and international exhibitions covering ancient marine reptiles and Wildlife Photographer of the Year, and has also scripted a Museum audio guide by Sir David Attenborough. An inquisitive Ravenclaw, Kate has a love of wolves and likes to celebrate the misunderstood or less charismatic creatures of our world. Her wand is carved from ebony wood with a phoenix-feather core and her Patronus is an Irish wolfhound.

THE NATURAL HISTORY MUSEUM

The Natural History Museum is one of the world's great museums and research institutions. It is the guardian of the UK's national collection of more than 80 million natural history specimens. Gathered over the last 400 years, the collections are vast and varied, ranging from whale skeletons, Martian meteorites, dinosaurs, spiders and everything in between. Many of the collections have great historical as well as scientific value, including those from Charles Darwin's voyage of the HMS *Beagle*, from which the theory of evolution was to emerge, and first ever discoveries from pioneering fossil collector Mary Anning.

The Natural History Museum's purpose is to inspire a love of our natural world and unlock answers to the big issues facing humanity and the planet. The Museum is home to more than 350 scientists who actively work with the collections and, by opening up access and participation for all, make it possible to address some of the big issues and challenges facing humanity and the planet, such as global loss of biodiversity and the impact of climate change, the security of our food supply and the eradication of disease.

THE EXHIBITION TEAM

Putting on an exhibition involves a huge team of people with a wide range of expertise and talents. From project managers and designers to conservators, registrars, photographers, engineers, mount-makers, filmmakers, audience researchers and special effects technicians, planning and delivering a project of this scale on time and on budget is only possible when well over a hundred people work together for a common goal.

A special mention goes to the over thirty Museum scientists who worked with the exhibition team to bring this exhibition to life. As well as giving access to the Museum's collections of mammals, birds, reptiles, fishes, insects and beyond, they contributed their specialist knowledge in selecting specimens for display and developing the science behind the stories.

J.K. Rowling is best known as the author of the seven Harry Potter books, which were published between 1997 and 2007. The enduringly popular adventures of Harry, Ron and Hermione have gone on to sell over 500 million copies, be translated into over 80 languages and made into eight blockbuster films. Alongside the Harry Potter series, she also wrote three short companion volumes for charity: *Quidditch Through the Ages* and *Fantastic Beasts and Where to Find Them*, in aid of Comic Relief and Lumos, and *The Tales of Beedle the Bard*, in aid of Lumos. J.K. Rowling collaborated with playwright Jack Thorne and director John Tiffany to continue Harry's story in a stage play, *Harry Potter and the Cursed Child*, which opened in London in 2016 and is now playing in Europe, North America and Australia. In the same year, she made her debut as a screenwriter with the film *Fantastic Beasts and Where to Find Them*, the first in a series featuring Magizoologist Newt Scamander, which was inspired by the original companion volume. J.K. Rowling has also written a standalone novel, *The Casual Vacancy*, and is the author of the Strike crime series under the pseudonym Robert Galbraith. Both have been adapted for television. She has received many awards and honours, including an OBE and a Companion of Honour for services to literature and philanthropy. She lives in Scotland with her family.

PICTURE CREDITS

WITH THANKS TO

Jim Kay and Olivia Lomenech Gill for allowing us to use their artwork;
Tomislav Tomic for creating new illustrations.

CONTRIBUTORS: Paul Ashman, Stephanie Clarkson,
Bronwyn O'Reilly and Claire Sipi;

Stephanie Amster, Jessica Bellman, Helen Chapman, Jessica George,
Sarah Goodwin, Claire Henry and Gemma Sharpe from Bloomsbury;

Louis Buckley, Lorraine Cornish, Anna Darron, Lucie Goodayle,
Kate Whittington and Colin Ziegler from the Natural History Museum;

Ross Fraser and Chloë Wallace from The Blair Partnership.

DESIGN: Dave Brown, Ape Inc Ltd
Stephanie Amster, Helen Chapman,
Scott Forsyth, Sarah Goodwin and Tom Hartley